# Leading Pharmaceutical Innovation

Oliver Gassmann · Gerrit Reepmeyer
Maximilian von Zedtwitz

# Leading Pharmaceutical Innovation

## Trends and Drivers for Growth
in the Pharmaceutical Industry

Second Edition

 Springer

Prof. Dr. Oliver Gassmann
Dr. Gerrit Reepmeyer
University of St. Gallen
Institute of Technology Management
Dufourstr. 40a
9000 St. Gallen
Switzerland
oliver.gassmann@unisg.ch
gerrit.reepmeyer@unisg.ch

Prof. Dr. Maximilian von Zedtwitz
AsiaCompete Int'l Ltd.
#1902 Wanguo Gongyue
18 Dongzhimenwai Xiaojie
100027 Beijing
PR China

max@post.harvard.edu

ISBN 978-3-540-77635-2          e-ISBN 978-3-540-77636-9

DOI 10.1007/978-3-540-77636-9

Library of Congress Control Number: 2007942737

*Production:* le-tex Jelonek, Schmidt & Vöckler GbR, Leipzig
*Cover design:* WMX Design GmbH, Heidelberg

Printed on acid-free paper

9 8 7 6 5 4 3 2 1

springer.com

# Preface for 2nd Edition

The importance of the topic has been reflected in the high demand for our first book. Since we finished the first edition, leading pharmaceutical companies seems to have become even more challenging in just a few years. Here are a few examples:

- **Double-digit industry growth has stopped to be a given fact.** While the pharmaceutical industry has historically been growing at an astounding annual rate of 11.1 percent from 1970 through 2002, projections for the future range somewhere between 5 to 8 percent per year globally. The industry leading giant Pfizer even had to post negative revenue growth for 2005 and 2006 respectively, for the first time in the firm's recent history. As a result, cost cutting programs – unthought-of in the late 1990s and early 2000s – have become a top priority on the agenda of many pharmaceutical executives.
- **The innovation productivity paradox has maintained its negative trend.** Worldwide industry spending on R&D continued to outpace new drug approvals. The major U.S. and European pharmaceutical companies spent a record amount of US$ 43 billion in 2006 to conduct research and development. However, only 29 new molecular entities have been approved by the FDA in the same year, compared to 53 just a decade ago. However, researchers produce more and more gene maps and pinpoint sources of our diseases and afflictions. While this is promising for mankind as a whole, it also puts extra expectations on pharmaceutical companies to turn this knowledge into new drugs. As much of this is done in public, pre-competitive research, it is available to competing firms as well.
- **Consolidation among major players to overcome growth and innovation productivity issues seems to have stagnated.** While the late 1990s and early 2000s saw multiple mega mergers (e.g., Pfizer and Warner-Lambert, Glaxo Wellcome and SmithKline Beecham, Pfizer and Pharmacia), pharmaceutical companies seem to prefer looser contractual agreements, such as collaborations and licensing deals to tackle today's most pressing issues. The total deal term value of collaborations in the pharmaceutical industry has almost tripled since 2000, reaching

over US$ 100 billion by 2004. Open innovation approaches – often cou-
pled with highly complex licensing agreements with various partners
across the entire pharmaceutical value chain – have become a common
phenomenon.

- **China makes an impact on the global life science scene.** Only since a
couple of years ago, global pharmaceutical firms set up research centers
in Shanghai, Beijing, and other Chinese cities. Chinese research institutes produce leading contributions to pharmaceutical research. China as
a market is undergoing a transition with its healthcare reform, and clinical development in a country with 300,000 hospitals and healthcare facilities appears very promising. No surprise that China already has about
6,800 domestic pharmaceutical companies fighting for market share.

- **Legal battles are testing the boundaries of responsibility in healthcare.** Several ongoing trials around drug safety issues in the pharmaceutical industry (e.g., the case of Vioxx) are a strong indicator for the dif-
ficulty to define the responsibilities of all stakeholders in the industry
regarding drug design, even long after drugs have been approved by the
FDA and are being prescribed by medical doctors. It becomes clear that
pharmaceutical innovation does not end with the completion of clinical
trials. To be successful, companies have to maneuver public opinion,
regulatory decisions, and financial markets alike. For example, Merck &
Co. has decided to fight the Vioxx battle case-by-case, and thereby
hopes to regain its position in the industry as well as reputation among
stakeholders.

- **The traditional pharmaceutical marketing model needs serious re-
consideration.** Sending thousands of sales representatives to high-
prescribing physicians to push potential blockbuster drugs on the market
doesn't seem to provide unique value any more. The trend towards
niche markets (e.g., specialty indications in oncology), increasing pressure from regulators, buyers and healthcare benefit organizations (e.g.,
reimbursement pressure, more powerful patient associations, consolidation among pharmacy benefit managers), the wide-spread availability of
information on treatment options (e.g., 'smarter' patients), as well as re-
tailers pushing for low-cost healthcare solutions (e.g., Wal-Mart's
US$ 4 generic drug prescription program) are all questioning the phar-
maceutical companies' ability to extract value from the pharmaceutical
value chain. Stagnating revenues along with stumbling share prices
seem to indicate that current approaches aren't appropriate to solve today's issues.

These are just *new* challenges adding themselves to those we have identified earlier, most fundamental among those probably the widening innovation productivity gap. While we again do not claim to have found the magic silver bullet that will solve all these problems, we have put in some effort to describe and analyze how industry leaders face up to these challenges, what tools they deploy, and what new solutions they are testing. Specifically, we have updated this second edition to include the latest technology and industry information, and we have paid particular attention to new management models such as open innovation, systematic partnering, out-licensing, and international diversification of R&D. This leads not just to new forms of collaboration in the pharmaceutical industry but also to new business models. We introduced a more balanced global perspective by reducing the focus on Switzerland as a lead country while adding more industry cases from the U.S. and Asia. All in all, this second edition is a fairly different book from the initial version just four years ago.

As the 2nd edition has been a real global project with distributed work around the globe, we hope that this edition gets the same global attention as the first one. Whether you are a pharmaceutical executive, an innovation researcher, a medical student, or a member of the general public genuinely interested in the pharmaceutical industry, we hope that each of you will join us in our appreciation for the tremendous work that is being done by the millions of people engaged in this industry with the respectable goal to provide mankind with better drugs and therapies to live and survive.

December 2007

St. Gallen                              Oliver Gassmann
New York                              Gerrit Reepmeyer
Beijing                                Maximilian von Zedtwitz

# Preface for 1ˢᵗ Edition

Pharmaceutical innovation is like gambling at roulette, only the stakes are higher. Considerably higher, since the most recent estimates put the costs of drug development at US$ 800 million to US$ 1 billion – per drug! This is equivalent to the price tag of the Empire State Building, when it was for sale a few years ago. In 2001, the major U.S. and European pharmaceutical companies invested more than US$ 30 billion in R&D, at a higher R&D-to-sales ratio than virtually any other industry, including chemicals, automobiles, electronics, aerospace, and computers.

Delivering a blockbuster drug is the Holy Grail for any pharmaceutical company. But in the last decade the rules of developing blockbusters seem to have changed. On the one hand, more sophisticated screening technologies, genetic engineering, and expanding networks with biotechnology companies increase the probability of commercial success. Critical success factors include the discovery phase and a stronger outside-in orientation in the early innovation phase. After the implosion of the high-tech stock market, biotechnology and other technology-driven opportunities may have lost some of their attractiveness for big pharma: a pipeline of solid and predictable innovations seems to be the highest goal of most pharmaceutical companies again. On the other hand, despite significant investments in pipeline management and novel technologies, there is still no recipe for ensuring a blockbuster hit. Instead, a disturbingly large number of blockbuster drugs were actually a result of serendipitous discoveries and unplanned spill-overs, such as the discovery of Viagra during blood-pressure related research. Despite decades of intensive research, we are still far away from being able to predict and measure the efficacy of pharmaceutical R&D.

So, is it 'back-to-basics' then? The three simplest but perhaps most difficult challenges that increase R&D productivity in pharmaceutical innovation are:

- Increasing the number of new and commercially successful products;
- Decreasing R&D and lifecycle costs;
- Decreasing development time.

'You can't manage what you can't measure', so goes an old managerial saying. In this book we are trying to develop a case for the manageability of pharmaceutical innovation despite its apparent lack of measurability. We understand pharmaceutical R&D management as vertically integrated activity which is not restricted to top management. As many scientists in research and almost all scientists in development are also managers, we would like to address them in their double roles of managerial decision makers and scientists.

Based on extensive research on innovation and R&D management in multinationals in several industries, we started to focus on the pharmaceutical industry in order to identify some key drivers and mechanisms of pharmaceutical R&D. Over the past years, but in particular in 2002 and 2003, we interviewed senior R&D and general managers of pharmaceutical companies around the world. We also did a fair share of background research such as studying intelligence reports, press releases, articles, publications, company presentations and searching the Internet. In second-round meetings we tested our hypotheses and theories, and we sharpened our examples and insights for managing R&D in the pharmaceutical industry. In addition, we conducted a workshop with 14 selected international experts on pharmaceutical R&D, during which we identified and consolidated new and emerging trends in pharmaceutical innovation.

We concentrated on Swiss pharmaceuticals for two reasons: Firstly, we had gathered substantial insight in the Swiss industry sector over the last few years while based at the University of St. Gallen and the Institute for Management Development in Lausanne. Swiss pharmaceutical companies were thus convenient yet also extremely telling examples. In fact, one chapter of this book was written around a study entitled 'Managing R&D in the Pharmaceutical Industry: The Case of Switzerland', which had been conducted for and financed by the Yokohama National University and the Health Care Science Institute in Tokyo (see also a Japanese translation of the report in the Journal of Health Care and Society, vol. 13, no. 2).

But more importantly, Switzerland assumes a unique role in pharmaceuticals worldwide. Nowhere else is the pharmaceutical industry's relative importance for the national economy as high as in Switzerland (in terms of contribution to GDP), and Swiss life science companies represent a surprisingly wide spectrum of the worldwide pharmaceutical and biotechnology industry within a relatively focused geographic area. We thus illustrate many of our findings with examples from the Swiss pharmaceutical industry. Also, we present two short case studies of the two largest Swiss pharmaceutical companies, Novartis and Hoffmann-La Roche, as an appendix to this book.

Few other industries are as driven by science, research and development as are pharmaceuticals. We therefore placed a deliberate emphasis on issues related to research and development within the wider realm of innovation. However, we also looked at other central areas of pharmaceutical innovation, such as the management of human resources, project and portfolio management and outsourcing. Moreover, the increasing importance of globalization in pharmaceutical science, technology and product development is covered in detail. This is also reflected in three core chapters of this book which are directly based on three key areas from which pharmaceutical companies expect major innovative developments to enhance innovation and productivity of pharmaceutical R&D:

- Novel R&D technologies, such as high-throughput screening and gene splicing;
- Reorganization and fine-tuning of R&D pipeline management;
- Outsourcing and internationalization of major phases of the R&D process, including basic research, candidate identification, and clinical development coordination.

These three themes are introduced in chapters 3, 4, and 5. Chapter 6 illustrates how some of the key management problems are dealt with by industry. We summarize our insights in a concluding chapter on perspectives and trends in pharmaceutical R&D and show some future directions for managing innovation in the pharmaceutical industry.

This book would not have been possible without the encouraging support of our research interviewees in various companies and their dedication to make sure that we understood the issues correctly. They spent valuable time sharing their thoughts and knowledge. In particular, we would like to thank Dr. Goetz Baumann, Marc Boivin, Jeff Butler, Dr. Gunter Festel, Dr. Urs Hofmeier, Dr. Marc Müller, Dr. Pius Renner, and Dr. Philipp Steiner. We are also grateful to Dr. Werner Müller of Springer for managing the overall publication process smoothly. Writing this book has been a great learning experience for us, and we hope the leading principles and examples of how to best manage pharmaceutical innovation included here are equally useful and inspiring to pharmaceutical managers and students of the pharmaceutical industry alike.

St. Gallen, Lausanne, Beijing                    Oliver Gassmann
                                                 Gerrit Reepmeyer
October 2003                                     Maximilian von Zedtwitz

# Contents

I.    Innovation: Key to Success in the Pharmaceutical Industry .......1
      The Productivity Paradox .................................................................1
      The Blockbuster Imperative .............................................................4
      High Risks in Drug Development .....................................................10
      Strategies for Growth .....................................................................12
      Differentiation via Clinical Profiles ................................................15
      Entering the Market Quickly ...........................................................16
      Conclusions .....................................................................................17

II.   The Industry Challenge: Do You Really Want to Be in This
      Business? .................................................................................19
      High Complexity of the Industry .....................................................19
      How Attractive is the Pharmaceutical Industry? .............................22
      Force 1: Bargaining Power of Suppliers...........................................24
      Force 2: Bargaining Power of Buyers .............................................25
      Force 3: Risk of Entry from Potential Competitors.........................26
      Force 4: Threat of Substitute Products ............................................27
      Force 5: Rivalry among Established Companies...............................28
      Force 6: The Regulators .................................................................28
      Conclusions .....................................................................................30

III.  The Science and Technology Challenge: How to Find New
      Drugs...........................................................................................33
      Rise of the Biotechnology Industry: Boosting Innovation ..............33
      High-Throughput Screening: Fail Earlier, Succeed Sooner ...........38
      Combinatorial Chemistry: Cut Experimental Cycle Times.............39
      Bioinformatics: More than 100 Gigabytes of Data per Day............40
      Proteomics: Profiting from the Human Genome Project..................42
      Genomics: Towards Individualization and Mass Customization ....43
      Pharmacogenomics: Create Tailor-made Drugs..............................45
      Molecular Design: From Experimenting to Analytic Design..........47
      Conclusions .....................................................................................48

**IV.  The Pipeline Management Challenge: How to Organize Innovation** ...................................................................**51**

The Relevance of Pipeline Management ......................................51
Complexity and Phases of the R&D Process................................56
The Importance of Project and Portfolio Management ...............65
The Disaggregation of the Pharmaceutical Value Chain.............68
Impact of Outsourcing on Pharmaceutical R&D..........................71
Rising Importance of R&D Collaborations ..................................75
Research Alliances: Accessing Early-stage Innovation ...............78
In-licensing: Enhancing the Innovation Pipeline.........................81
Co-development: Mutually Benefiting from Joint Resources ........83
Out-licensing: Commercializing Internal Research Results...........86
How to Commercialize a Breakthrough Technology .....................95
Conclusions ................................................................................100

**V.   The Internationalization Challenge: Where to Get Access to Innovation** ..............................................................................**103**

Trends and Drivers of R&D Internationalization .........................103
Primary Locations of Pharmaceutical R&D around the World.....108
New Opportunities for Drug Development in China.....................111
Three Principal Problems of Dispersed R&D ..............................117
Conclusions ................................................................................121

**VI.  Management Answers to Pharmaceutical R&D Challenges ...123**

Managing R&D Organization at Roche ......................................123
Managing R&D Strategy at Schering...........................................125
Managing the Research-to-Development Handover at Roche ......127
Managing Outsourcing Activities at Solvias ...............................130
Managing Intellectual Property Rights at Bayer ..........................133
Managing Out-licensing at Novartis............................................137
Managing Uncertainty at Roche .................................................144
Managing Global R&D at Major Swiss Pharma Companies ........145
Managing a Niche-Market Strategy at Intarcia ...........................151
Managing Virtual Project Management Pools at Roche................153
Conclusions ................................................................................156

**VII. Future Directions and Trends** .................................................**159**

Bibliography ........................................................................165
Index ..................................................................................173
Glossary ............................................................................179
Authors ..............................................................................185

# I.  Innovation: Key to Success in the Pharmaceutical Industry

*"The next ten years will be seen as a signal point of transition in healthcare. Medicine will be transformed from an instinctive art of alleviating symptoms to a science of personalized healthcare. The next decade will be viewed by future generations as the time when treatments became preventative, predictive, and personalized."*

*Michael Leavitt,*
*Secretary of the U.S. Department of Health and Human Services*

## The Productivity Paradox

Despite its high R&D intensity, the pharmaceutical industry is facing an increasingly dire situation. On average, only 1 out of 10,000 substances becomes a marketable product. And only 3 out of 10 drugs generate revenues that meet or exceed average R&D costs (see Grabowski, Vernon, DiMasi 2002).

By definition, R&D productivity is the ratio of input in R&D versus its output. The black-box in between consists of the drug development pipeline, new screening and research technologies, worldwide cooperation networks in clinical research and testing, and a whole new armada of licensing and cooperation agreements with universities, competitors and biotechnology start-ups. Still, as a Reuters study (2003a) shows, R&D performance of the major pharmaceutical companies is sub-optimal:

- Pipeline output is low and declining;
- Costs of R&D are rising rapidly, driven by larger and more complex clinical studies and expensive new enabling technologies;

- Over-supply of 'me-too' launches and a lack of genuinely innovative drugs make it difficult to replace revenues lost through patent expiry;
- Protracted clinical trials and administrative procedures reduce the marketed shelf life of patented products.

R&D expenditures account for a large share of the overall cost structure in the pharmaceutical industry. As the effective cost structure of an original product may vary considerably depending on the therapeutic area served, generalizations about fixed percentage levels for the various cost factors cannot be made. Hence, the following table cites ranges rather than exact figures. A large proportion of the margin is reinvested in new drug R&D.

**Table 1.** Average cost structure of a newly developed drug.

| Relative Contribution | Cost Factors |
|---|---|
| 20% - 40% | Research, Development, Licenses |
| 15% - 30% | Production |
| 5% - 15% | Technical and Administrative Costs |
| 20% - 30% | Marketing and Distribution |
| 20% - 35% | Margin |

Source: Pharma Information (2002)

In addition, R&D expenditures of pharmaceutical companies worldwide have grown constantly over the last decades (in relative terms, from 11.4 percent of sales in 1970 to 18.5 percent in 2001), and according to PhRMA (2007), the major U.S. and European pharmaceutical companies invested US$ 43 billion in R&D in 2006. But since the mid-1990s, the launch of new drugs on the market has declined or has been constant at best (Fig. 1). The number of new molecular entities (NMEs) approved by the Food and Drug Administration (FDA) in the United States fell from 53 in 1996 to just 29 in 2006.

Consequently, drug development costs per new drug approval are constantly increasing. In 1976, it cost US$ 54 million to develop a new drug, US$ 231 million in 1987, and about US$ 280 million in 1991 (DiMasi 2001). This number has grown to almost US$ 1.5 billion by now (see Fig. 1). Even though it is not legitimate to make a direct comparison between R&D spending and R&D productivity, the tendency of increasing R&D costs per drug is certainly a concern with top management in pharmaceutical companies.

Furthermore, the average duration of drug development has increased significantly over the last decades. The average time a drug candidate

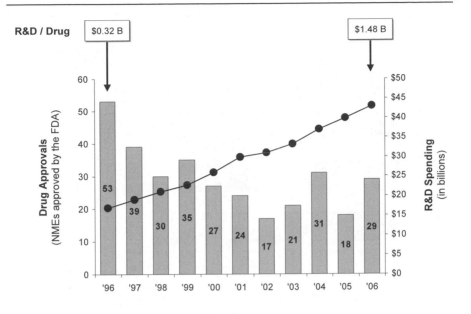

Source: PhRMA (2007)

**Fig. 1.** The productivity gap in pharmaceutical research and development.

spends in clinical trials has increased from 2.8 years in the mid-1960s to 6.6 years by the 1990s. However, it seems to have leveled off in the 2000s (see Fig. 2). Modest time gains seem to have been made mostly during the drug approval stage (i.e. after most R&D has actually been completed) and where the cooperation and involvement of regulatory authorities is paramount.

A significant increase in productivity in pharmaceutical innovation is needed in order to close the widening productivity gap and to meet the high revenue growth expectations of the industry. This seems like a tall order, given that most mature industries have not grown by more than 1-2 percent over the past years. Only the fastest growing economy in the world, China, has grown by more than 8 percent in the same period.

In the pharmaceutical industry, however, worldwide sales have grown at a historical annual rate of 11.1 percent from 1970 until 2002 (PhRMA 2003). Today, these double-digit growth rates are strictly incorporated into the industry's overall growth expectations. As success raises stakeholders' expectations of further success, pharmaceutical companies are forced primarily by investors and management to at least maintain this growth rate for the foreseeable future. The winners in the pharmaceutical industry even

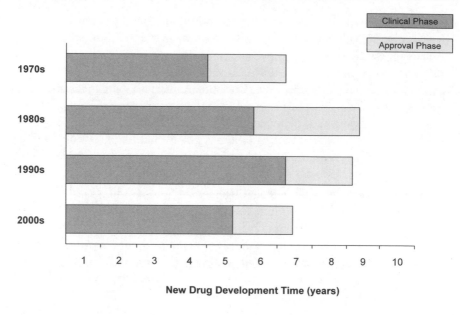

Source: PhRMA (2004)

**Fig. 2.** Time spent by a drug candidate in the clinical and approval phases.

have to exceed these growth expectations in order to deliver above-average returns to their shareholders. For the past decades, the silver bullet for achieving these growth rates has been the blockbuster model.

## The Blockbuster Imperative

Reliance on blockbuster drugs – a drug with at least US\$ 1 billion in annual revenues – has remained a largely unquestioned growth strategy of most leading pharmaceutical companies, and is often quoted as the only viable way to meet the high growth expectations. One reason is that blockbuster drugs offer relatively high returns compared to lower value drugs, due to the substantial risks, time and costs involved in product development and commercialization. In addition, developing drugs with blockbuster potential is a more sustainable growth strategy than relying on patent defense.

In 2002, 58 ethical pharmaceutical products have been considered blockbuster drugs. Cumulatively, they represented more than US\$ 120 billion in sales, the equivalent of almost half of the global pharmaceutical market at that time (Reuters 2003a).

However, problems experienced by companies like Pfizer, Merck and Schering-Plough, both of which are/have been heavily reliant on block-buster revenues but are now facing patent expiration and maturing drug portfolios, raise the question of whether blockbusters can or should remain a focus of future growth. The emergence and growing power of generic companies, such as the Israeli company Teva Pharmaceuticals, pose an increasing threat to established pharmaceutical companies. Some ethical drugs might loose up to 80 percent in market share within just one quarter after patent expiration, exposing several US$ billions worth in revenues to generic competition.

Looking forward, the blockbuster market in 2008 is expected to be worth only 1.4 times that of the blockbuster market in 2000. Thus, companies are not able to keep up with double-digit revenue growth expectations by simply relying on blockbuster drugs. A company generating US$ 30 billion of revenues in 2000 must increase its sales by an additional US$ 23 billion by 2008 if its investors' 10%+ annual revenue growth expectations are to be achieved. Therefore, a US$ 1 billion product in 2000 will need to be a US$ 1.8 billion product in 2008. While in the first half of 2002, 53 products with the potential to generate annual sales of US$ 1 billion or

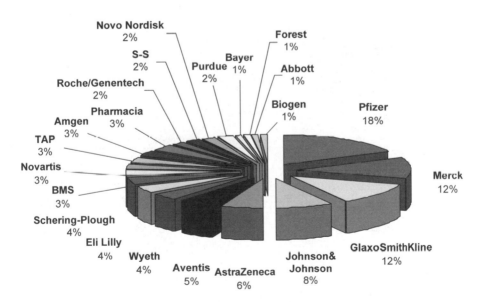

Source: Reuters (2003a)

**Fig. 3.** Share of the global blockbuster market by company in 2002.

more in 2008 were identified, only 21 of these were considered to have the ability to exceed US$ 1.8 billion (Reuters 2003a). Thus, the requirements of blockbuster products – to reach almost US$ 2 billion in annual sales – will be increasingly hard to accomplish in the future.

In 2002, 24 companies were responsible for marketing the 58 block-buster drugs. The most successful company was Pfizer owning about 18 percent of the worldwide blockbuster market (see Fig. 3). In 2003, Pfizer's blockbuster Lipitor had become the first pharmaceutical product ever that exceeded annual sales of more than US$ 10 billion. Today, Lipitor still generates a whopping US$ 13 billion in revenues for Pfizer, but its nearing patent expiration causes great concern for Pfizer, especially when it is considered that development of Lipitor's follow-on product needed to be stopped last year due to efficacy problems.

However, with individual company blockbuster sales ranging from just over US$ 1 billion to more than US$ 22 billion, and blockbuster growth rates varying from -28 percent to more than 45 percent, there are clearly considerable variations in the dynamics of the blockbuster market (Fig. 4). In this historical blockbuster comparison, Pfizer topped the list as the most successful company between 2001 and 2002 with blockbuster sales of

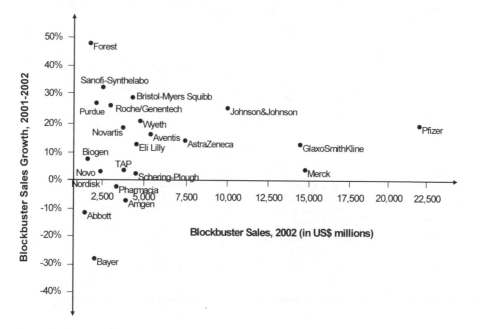

Source: Reuters (2003a)

**Fig. 4.** Historical blockbuster sales and sales growth by company from 2001-2002.

more than US$ 22 billion and a blockbuster sales growth rate of about 20 percent. Merck and GlaxoSmithKline with about US$ 15 billion in blockbuster sales came in second and third. Bayer owned just one blockbuster product at that time and reported a significantly negative blockbuster sales growth during the same time period.

The 10 best selling blockbuster products of today including their indication, marketing company, therapy area and sales are listed in the following table.

**Table 2.** Global blockbuster products in 2006.

| # | Brand | Indication | Company | Sales [*] | Therapy Area |
|---|-------|-----------|---------|-----------|--------------|
| 1 | Lipitor | Hyper-cholesterolemia | Pfizer | 13,633 | Cardiovascular |
| 2 | Seretide, Advair | Asthma; COPD | GlaxoSmith-Kline | 6,618 | Pulmonary & respiratory |
| 3 | Plavix, Iscover | Thrombosis | Sanofi-Aventis, BMS | 6,290 | Small molecule |
| 4 | Epogen, Procrit | Renal and cancer anemia | Amgen, Johnson & Johnson | 5,691 | Renal & oncology |
| 5 | Nexium | Gastroesophageal reflux disease (GERD) | AstraZeneca | 5,182 | Gastro-intestinal |
| 6 | Norvasc | Hypertension | Pfizer | 4,866 | Cardiovascular |
| 7 | Enbrel | Rheumatoid arthritis; psoriasis, etc. | Amgen, Wyeth, Takeda | 4,475 | Inflammation |
| 8 | Risperdal, Consta | Schizophrenia | Johnson & Johnson | 4,184 | Neurology & psychiatry |
| 9 | Aranesp | Renal and cancer anemia | Amgen | 4,121 | Renal & oncology |
| 10 | Rituxan, MabThera | B-cell lymphoma | Roche (Biogen) | 3,912 | Oncology |

* in US$ million

Source: La Merie (2007)

In 2002, only two companies – GlaxoSmithKline and Pfizer – owned eight blockbuster products. The majority of companies owned between one and three blockbusters (see Fig. 5). Companies, such as Pfizer, Merck, Biogen, or TAP, depend very much on their blockbuster products. Blockbusters were responsible for the majority of ethical sales by contributing between 70 and 90 percent to total revenues. Firms with a more diversified product portfolio include, for example, Abbott, Bayer or Novartis.

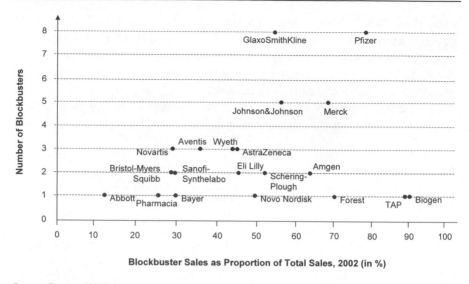

Source: Reuters (2003a)

**Fig. 5.** Contribution of blockbuster sales to ethical sales in 2002.

The blockbuster market is mainly dominated by cardiovascular and central nervous system (CNS) therapies (Fig. 6). In fact, with combined sales of more than US$ 57 billion in 2002, they represent nearly half of all blockbuster sales (i.e., 27 and 21 percent respectively). Other major therapy areas of today's blockbuster products include gastrointestinal (9%), respiratory (9%), infectious disease (8%), and adjunct therapy (7%).

Underpinning blockbuster success in the cardiovascular and CNS markets is a substantial patient population and a high degree of unmet need. More than 300 million people in the seven major national markets (US, UK, Japan, France, Germany, Italy, Spain) suffer from the most common form of dyslipidemia, hypercholesterolemia, making it one of the most prevalent conditions in the Western world (Reuters 2003a).

Three of the top five cardiovascular blockbusters are anti-dyslipidemics; Pfizer's Lipitor (atorvastatin), Merck's Zocor (simvastatin), and Bristol-Myers Squibb's Pravachol (pravastatin). While these markets may seem attractive due to their enormous size, competition has become fierce. Only with highly intensive marketing support, Pfizer was able to turn Lipitor into the most lucrative pharmaceutical product of all time.

Sales growth of cardiovascular and CNS blockbusters has been driven primarily by the increasing success of existing rather than new blockbusters, although a small number of products enjoyed their first year as block-

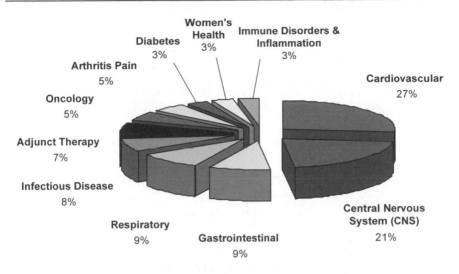

Source: Reuters (2003a)

**Fig. 6.** Segmentation of the global blockbuster market by therapy area in 2002.

buster drugs in 2002, including Johnson&Johnson's pain patch, Duragesic (fentanyl), and Novartis' anti-hypertensive Lotensin/Lotrel (benazepril).

According to their respective growth potential, the therapeutic areas of the blockbuster market can be differentiated between stable and emerging blockbusters (see Table 3).

**Table 3.** Classification of therapeutic areas and blockbuster markets according to Reuters.

| Stable Blockbuster Markets | Emerging Blockbuster Markets |
| --- | --- |
| Gastrointestinal | Adjunct therapy |
| Respiratory | Oncology |
| Infectious disease | Arthritis pain |
| Women's health | Diabetes |
| | Immune disorders & inflammation |

Source: Reuters (2003a)

Stable markets are already served by highly effective drugs that treat large patient populations. Their levels of unmet therapeutic need are typically lower than in the cardiovascular and CNS areas, resulting in lower blockbuster growth rates. Sectors classified as emerging blockbuster markets are characterized by a high level of unmet therapeutic need. In gen-

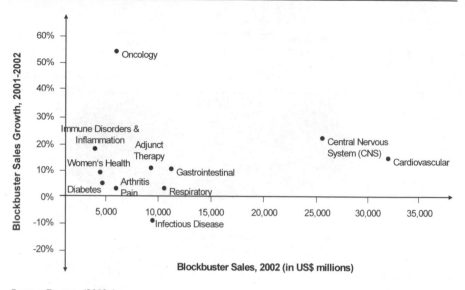

Source: Reuters (2003a)

**Fig. 7.** Blockbuster sales and growth by therapy area from 2001-2002.

eral, their growth is driven by the introduction of selective products that offer high efficacy and response rates.

Reflecting respective market sizes and growth rates, the therapeutic areas can be classified according to their overall attractiveness as measured by their revenue and sales potential (Fig. 7).

## High Risks in Drug Development

In addition to its dependence on a few high-volume products, the pharmaceutical industry is characterized by another unique circumstance. In most industries, the decision to terminate an R&D project is made on the basis of economic/financial considerations; in the pharmaceutical industry, however, most R&D projects are dropped due to scientific reasons, such as a lack of efficacy or safety that might only become visible at late clinical stages.

Due to the surge in the average R&D costs per new drug approval, any failure of a newly developed substance during the R&D process causes significant losses. Thus, the attrition rates in drug development (i.e. the percentage of substances in development that drop out during a phase of testing) expose pharmaceutical companies to tremendous risks. In fact, any

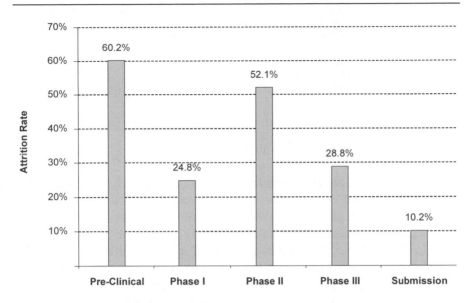

Source: Buchanan (2002) based on The Tufts Center for Drug Development data

**Fig. 8.** Attrition rates in pharmaceutical R&D by phase.

adverse news about a new compound in development can cause share prices of pharmaceutical companies to drop significantly, destroying several US$ billions in shareholder value within minutes.

The bad news is that attrition rates in pharmaceutical R&D are fairly high, particularly at late stages of the development process. Drug development attrition rates are highest in the pre-clinical phase (60.2%) and still very high in clinical phase II (52.1%), that is after several years of development have already been conducted (see Fig. 8).[*] Once a new drug candidate has been submitted to the regulatory authorities for approval, the attrition rate decreases to around 10 percent.

Translating the attrition rates into success rates provides an overview about the probability of success for a compound in the R&D pipeline to reach the market. While a compound in the pre-clinical phase only has a probability to reach the market of around 10 percent, this rate increases significantly once the compound passes the clinical Phase II and reaches clinical Phase III (65.8%). Considering and comparing attrition rates and probabilities of success, the greatest potential for improvement in productivity seems to be in clinical phase II as well as just before the pre-clinical phase (i.e. lead identification and lead optimization).

---

[*] Chapter IV provides a detailed overview of the different phases in drug development.

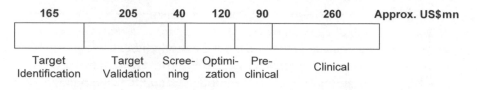

| 165 | 205 | 40 | 120 | 90 | 260 | Approx. US$mn |
|-----|-----|-----|-----|-----|-----|-----|
| Target Identification | Target Validation | Scree-ning | Optimi-zation | Pre-clinical | Clinical | |

Source: BCG (2001)

**Fig. 9.** Breakdown of drug R&D expenditures.

Particularly the high attrition rates in clinical phase II directly translate into significant R&D risks. The later a project is cancelled, the more resources have been allocated and the higher the respective financial loss. A drug candidate that reached clinical phase II has already dissipated more than US$ 600-700 millions on average (see Fig. 9). If a drug's efficacy and safety for the desired indication cannot be assured during the late clinical stages, the compound's development usually has to be stopped, no matter if these huge research and development efforts have been made so far.

## Strategies for Growth

Given the rising costs and surging risks in drug development, the pharmaceutical industry still posts solid growth rates of around 5-8 percent per year. Subsequently, the following question arises: Where does growth in the pharmaceutical market come from? According to a study by IMS Health in the year 2000, drug spending increased by 18.8 percent in 1999. The lion's share (10.8%) is derived from increased utilization, 4.2 percent is accounted for by price inflation, and only 3.8 percent comes from truly new medicines, that is pharmaceutical innovation.

Usage, prices, and applications of drugs are influenced by a great number of stakeholders in the pharmaceutical industry, as we will see below. While overall healthcare costs are increasing, a series of studies by Lichtenberg (1996, 2000) showed that increased spending on prescription drugs actually leads to overall decreases in healthcare spending. He found that a reduction of US$ 71 in non-drug spending was accompanied by an US$ 18 increase in newer prescription drugs, resulting in net savings of US$ 53.

Prices are typically strongly regulated by federal governments. Because of the critical situation of the healthcare sectors in most developed countries, we have seen administrators use a blanket approach to curb healthcare costs, ignoring the potentially compensating effects of new drug use as described by Lichtenberg (2000). Additionally, growth from new applications and customers has limited potential in saturated markets and markets with low purchasing power such as developing countries. Pharmaceutical innovation and the number of new products will have to increase in order to sustain growth.

From a company's perspective, growth in market share can also be achieved externally: A few pharmaceutical companies have made headlines because of recent merger & acquisition (M&A) activity. The most recent examples of mergers include Bayer & Schering AG, Schering-Plough & Organon or Sanofi-Synthélabo & Aventis. Still, the industry has further M&A potential and is far from consolidation: Reflecting that the overall pharmaceutical market in 2006 reached about US$ 650 billion in sales, the top 10 companies in aggregation only owned around 50 percent of the market (see Table 4).

**Table 4.** Top 20 pharmaceutical companies in the world in 2006.

| Rank | Company | Country | Revenues[*] |
|------|---------|---------|-------------|
| 1 | Pfizer | US | 48.4 |
| 2 | GlaxoSmithKline | UK | 42.8 |
| 3 | Novartis | CH | 37.0 |
| 4 | Sanofi-Aventis | F | 35.6 |
| 5 | Roche | CH | 34.0 |
| 6 | AstraZeneca | UK | 26.5 |
| 7 | Johnson & Johnson | US | 23.2 |
| 8 | Merck & Co. | US | 22.6 |
| 9 | Abbott Laboratories | US | 22.6 |
| 10 | Wyeth | US | 20.4 |
| 11 | Bayer | GER | 18.2 |
| 12 | Bristol-Myers Squibb | US | 17.9 |
| 13 | Eli Lilly | US | 15.7 |
| 14 | Amgen | US | 14.3 |
| 15 | Boehringer Ingelheim | GER | 13.3 |
| 16 | Schering-Plough | US | 10.6 |
| 17 | Baxter International | US | 10.4 |
| 18 | Takeda Pharmaceutical Co. | JP | 10.3 |
| 19 | Genentech | US | 9.3 |
| 20 | Procter & Gamble | US | 9.0 |

* in US$ billions, only includes sales of pharmaceutical products

Source: MedAdNews (2007)

Why do companies merge? One of the most frequently offered reasons for mergers is the exploitation of synergy effects, resulting in the reduction of costs in administration, sales, and development. Another reason is the access to new markets and industry subsectors. Thus, it is claimed that 'added value can be generated for investors'.

Mega-mergers do not necessarily result in higher market share or greater productivity, as illustrated by a Wood Mackenzie (2003a) study. Grouping the top 10 pharmaceutical companies in 'mega-merged companies' (Pfizer, GSK, BMS, Aventis, Novartis, Pharmacia) and 'non-mega-merged companies' (Merck, J&J, Eli Lilly, Roche), the study found that between 1995 and 2002, 'mega-merged companies' lost on average 2.8 percent of their worldwide share in the ethical drug market, while 'non-mega-merged companies' won 10 percent. They also found that 'mega-merged companies' appear to produce fewer NCEs after their mergers than before (see Fig. 10).

Why do mergers remain attractive? Pharmaceutical companies pursue a mix of defensive and aggressive growth strategies. Defensive strategies aim to retain a competitive position by means of co-marketing agreements, co-selling, cross-licensing, and market-related acquisitions among others. This strategy builds critical size and momentum, reduces costs of sales, and essentially creates entry barriers for newcomers. Aggressive strategies try to overcome entry barriers set up by competitors: companies develop and apply new technologies, complex knowledge and project portfolio management (the pipeline), pursue outsourcing and internationalization. While this strategy does not immediately reduce overall costs, it does pro-

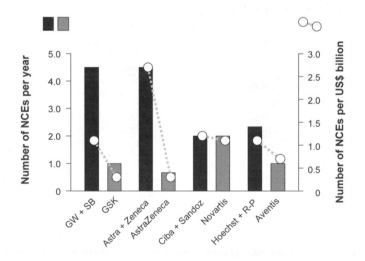

Source: Wood Mackenzie (2003a)

**Fig. 10.** R&D productivity (measured in NCEs decreased in top 10 pharmaceutical companies) 3 years before and 3 years after the merger.

vide a greater potential for creating value-added and hence long-term cost reduction.

Some companies pursue a balanced strategy of both approaches, whereas others seem to have made a choice. In this book, we focus more on the latter type of strategies.

## Differentiation via Clinical Profiles

> *"Like it or not: Cost effectiveness of medical interventions will become a decisive factor for market success. Only true innovations that create an incremental benefit, i.e. a better or longer life, will be rewarded with top dollars."*
>
> *Wolfgang Renner,*
> *CEO, Cyots Biotechnology*

The most sustainable approach to create value in pharmaceutical innovation seems to be simple: offer a drug with a superior clinical profile compared to competitors' drugs. However, achieving this objective turns out to be fairly difficult in reality. A drug's clinical profile is regarded as one of the most influential predictors of its commercial success. In general, a drug's clinical profile consists of four major criteria (see Reuters 2003a):

- Efficacy;
- Safety/side effects;
- Dosage/administration;
- Costs.

In other words, if a product is efficacious, has negligible side effects and can be administered with a convenient dosing mechanism, it is in a good position to compete in most markets. The degree to which a product can be differentiated by any or all of these criteria varies by therapeutic market and competitive environment. For example, late market entrants offering only marginal improvements in efficacy may need to enhance their commercial prospects by competing on the basis of a lower price. Alternatively, trials can be designed to target areas of unmet need, for example efficacy in specific patient subpopulations or improved dosage schedules.

Clinical trial data are typically generated during the drug's development in the clinical phases I to III. As the pressure for product differentiation has significantly increased in the pharmaceutical industry, it is increasingly common for companies to conduct phase IV trials after a product has been launched. Such trials typically focus on further indications and subpopulations or seek to differentiate a product from its major competitors through head-to-head studies. Once valuable trial data has been generated, it is important to convey the information to key audiences, particularly opinion leaders and high prescribing physicians, in such a way that a product's benefits relative to its competitors are clear. In addition to a drug's profile, timing of market entry is another critical success factor.

## Entering the Market Quickly

The growth rate and market share gained in the first year after a drug's launch largely determine overall sales that can subsequently be achieved for any newly introduced product (Reuters 2003a). Time-to-market is extremely important in breakthrough pharmaceuticals. The first in the market captures between 40 to 60 percent of the market, and the second only around 15 percent. Coming in third already means a negative business. Moreover, delaying market introduction of a blockbuster drug by two months not only involves the risk that a competitor seizes significant market share, it also means a net loss of US$ 100 million, or almost US$ 2 million a day. Consequently, the first year of a drug's marketed life attracts the majority of promotional resources relative to any other year in the life-cycle.

Numerous products including Pfizer's blockbuster Lipitor illustrate this pattern. All of these products experienced above average sales growth in their first year on the market and have since continued to display strong sales performances. Although there are cases where first year market performance was good but sales did not meet long-term expectations, this is usually due to a major external event, for example the discovery of major negative side-effects.

The market dynamics during the product launch are characterized by three closely-linked determinants. To improve the probability of a new drug turning out to be a success, the product should be (see Reuters 2003a):

- Early to enter a particular therapy area or product class;
- Positioned relative to existing competition;
- Accompanied by heightened pre-launch awareness.

Notably, pre-launch promotion has become more important in recent years. A new product's rate of acceptance can be significantly boosted if the market is well prepared for it. The key focus of such investments is raising awareness among physicians and, eventually, patients. This is particularly important in new areas when a product is first to market or if there is little awareness of the disease, its symptoms and treatment options.

Marketing departments are working increasingly close with their R&D counterparts to ensure that clinical trials are designed to meet specific market needs and that this is conveyed to physicians prior to launch. To this end, developing and nurturing relationships with physician opinion leaders throughout the R&D process is critical. Firstly, this helps determine unmet market needs, clinical trial design and product positioning. Secondly, and most crucially in the context of market penetration, such relationships drive product uptake upon launch, as opinion leaders will already be familiar with the product and its benefits (see Reuters 2003a).

Pre-launch marketing activities often include establishing advisory boards and sponsoring pre-launch conferences at which clinical trial results are presented to the wider medical community. However, they also include the direct involvement of leading physicians and medical establishments in clinical trials. By convincing opinion leaders of a drug's benefits, acceptance among late adopters can be accelerated. Early product branding further raises awareness among physicians prior to launch, increasing the likelihood of higher levels of initial uptake.

Raising pre-launch awareness also ensures that the needs of all stakeholders in the prescribing process are addressed before a product is launched. The payers' needs should also be considered as they have the final word on price and reimbursement levels.

Even though pharmaceutical companies do not necessarily need to raise awareness of a product with payers in the same way as with physicians and patients, pre-launch preparation should include health economics and outcomes studies (e.g., cost-effectiveness studies) to demonstrate product value to payers. This is particularly important in publicly funded healthcare systems operating under extensive cost containment policies.

## Conclusions

New markets are either not willing to pay the high prices common in the U.S. and most European countries, or these markets are highly uncertain, difficult and expensive to develop. One new market in the U.S. and European economies, for example, is geriatrics. People are becoming increasingly old, while at the same time healthcare spending is increasing with age. For instance, average U.S. Medicaid prescription drug spending was US$ 358 per enrollee, while the group of elderly accounted for about US$

893 in drug spending per enrollee. Thus, there are many new medicines under development that specifically aim at treating older people, targeting diseases such as diabetes, rheumatoid arthritis, Alzheimer's, depression, gastrointestinal disorders, osteoporosis, bladder/kidney disorders, or Parkinson's disease.

Focusing on blockbusters appears to be an enviable competitive position, given the strong first-mover advantages in the pharmaceutical market. However, if a significant share of total sales depends on blockbusters, a company exposes itself to the risk of sharp sales drops once the underlying drug loses patent protection. Most pharmaceutical companies have thus started to balance and hedge their drug portfolios more rigorously.

# II. The Industry Challenge: Do You Really Want to Be in This Business?

*"Longer term, I am convinced that societies will see the special value and benefit of pharmaceutical innovation. We'll be a healthy, vibrant industry for the future."*

Fred Hassan,
Chairman, CEO and President, Schering-Plough

## High Complexity of the Industry

The pharmaceutical industry used to be the cash cow in many countries. Profitable business and shareholder value seemed to be guaranteed. But the attractiveness of this industry has changed due to dynamic forces in the competitive as well as regulatory environment. Product quality concerns and ensuing legal battles turned pharmaceutical companies even more cautious about launching new drugs, as even large venerable firms have been brought close to complete collapse in the wake of Vioxx and other events. The meteoric rise of China in the manufacturing and electronics industry hasn't even started in the pharmaceutical industry, but its antecedents are clearly influencing decision making in the international community already. What used to be an already highly complex industry has become even more complex. Maneuvering this industry is becoming increasingly difficult.

## Industry classification and background

Originally, the pharmaceutical industry emerged from the chemical industry. Still today, chemistry represents a significant part in the innovation of pharmaceutical products. There are a number of similarities in the production processes of both chemical and pharmaceutical substances, and many industry experts aggregate the chemical and the pharmaceutical industries into one single industry called 'the pharmaceutical-chemical industry'. However, despite of the similarities between chemicals and pharmaceuticals, there has been a general trend towards their separation into independent disciplines. Although there are still many companies that operate a pharmaceutical division side to side with a chemical division, capital markets have increasingly favored firms that separated these businesses. The reasons are found in higher profitability and lower exposure to cyclic trends in the pharmaceutical industry, which leads to a stronger shareholder value orientation.

Today, pharmaceuticals are usually aggregated – along with the product groups of vitamins, fine chemicals, plant protection agents and animal medicine – under the broader category of so-called life science products (i.e., products that intervene in the metabolic processes of living organisms). Including specialty chemicals, the different product categories can be characterized as follows:

- The pharmaceuticals product group mainly includes patented, innovative products available only by prescription of a physician (either patented or generic). Over-the-counter (OTC) drugs and diagnostic aids have recently increased in importance as well.
- The product group of plant protection agents includes herbicides, fungicides and insecticides. The animal medicines group includes drugs for pets and livestock.
- The vitamins and fine chemicals product group includes the 13 vitamins and their derivatives as well as flavors and fragrances. These are not products for direct consumption, but rather 'bulk products' that are used for manufacturing pharmaceuticals, foodstuffs and animal feed.

The specialty chemicals product group comprises of a number of highly specialized products that are frequently manufactured in relatively small quantities in response to specific needs of individual customers. With these products, professional advice to customers is a rule of considerable importance.

The pharmaceuticals product group can be broken down further into several product groups that may address various different therapeutic areas. The classification according to therapeutic areas is also often the basis for the organizational structure in most pharmaceutical companies.

## Extensive product groups

Pharmaceutical products are defined as 'substances or mixtures of substances, which are meant for use in the recognition, prevention or treatment of diseases or for some other medical purposes regarding influences on the human organism' (Leutenegger 1994). In general, drugs are differentiated into prescription drugs and non-prescription drugs. Further drug classifications include generic drugs, diagnostic drugs, orphan drugs or genetically manufactured drugs.

**Prescription drugs** are also often referred to as ethical drugs. They are only distributed by pharmacies or hospitals after they have been prescribed by a physician. In some cases, the physicians are also allowed to distribute prescription drugs themselves. These so-called self-dispensing physicians are very common, for example, in the Swiss pharmaceutical market. They do not just prescribe the respective drug, they also dispense the product. Recently, the Swiss Association of Physicians with their own Dispensary (Vereinigung der Ärzte mit Patientenapotheke) started to prefer the term 'Direct Dispensing of Medicines' (Direkte Medikamentenabgabe, DMA) instead of 'Self-dispensing' (see Pharma Information 2002).

**Non-prescription drugs** can usually be purchased over-the-counter (OTC) at pharmacies and drugstores, or can be obtained in hospitals. Hence, non-prescription drugs include both medicines bought in pharmacies and drugstores without a prescription and medicines prescribed in medical practices and hospitals (see Pharma Information 2001). OTC drugs are also sometimes referred to as drugs purely used for self-medication purposes (i.e., without any prescription at all). OTC drugs are usually used for minor ailments such as headache or the flu.

**Generic drugs** are replications of prescription or non-prescription drugs where the patent protection has expired. Therefore, generic drugs (also referred to as generics) are usually offered by firms that did not develop the drugs themselves but gained a license to sell the drug. As these firms do not have to recoup high R&D expenditures, generic drugs are usually marketed at a much lower price than the original drug, but they have the same efficacy because they use the same underlying substances as the original patent protected drug used to do. Drugs that are about to lose their patent protection are thus exposed to severe competition. For instance, Eli Lilly's historic growth driver Prozac lost U.S. patent protection in August 2001, and consequently, its sales declined by 66 percent in the fourth quarter of 2001 as a result of generic competition. Responding to the generic challenge, many pharmaceutical companies have started their own generics business. Novartis generics business (operated under the brand name Sandoz) has become one of the largest generics businesses in the world, and is one of Novartis' growth drivers today.

**Orphan drugs** target rare medical conditions with usually very low patient populations. Thus, they provide physicians with therapeutic alternatives, and in some cases, they even provide a first therapeutic option. The FDA grants orphan drug status to a company for a drug that is believed to substantially increase the life expectancy of the treated patient for a particular disease. This excludes other companies from receiving an FDA license to produce a similar drug for a finite period (usually 7 years), thereby allowing the company producing the drug to recuperate their R&D expenses. For the pharmaceutical and biotech companies involved, the advantages are less apparent, although legislation in markets such as the US, Japan, Canada, Australia and now Europe provides financial and development support to manufacturers. However, a company developing an orphan drug cannot expect to generate enormous profits due to the small size of the target markets, and the risks involved are still substantial. Hence, orphan drug legislation has consistently been perceived as being of principle advantage to the consumer. Besides of providing exclusivity in a particular indication area or benefiting from other leveraging effects, orphan drugs can be used to improve the public profile of a company. In fact, the number of orphan drug applications has started to increase in the last decade. Between 1995 and 2005, a total number of 160 orphan drugs had been approved.

**Genetically manufactured drugs** play an increasingly important role in the pharmaceutical pipeline. Gene technology includes all methods to characterize and utilize genetic material and is used for drug discovery, research simulation, and even diagnostic purposes. The limitations of gene technology are mostly ethical.

## How Attractive is the Pharmaceutical Industry?

Considering the strong dependence on innovation and growth, the high risks in research and development as well as the high complexity of its products, it might be reasonable to ask the question: How attractive is the pharmaceutical industry overall?

This question cannot be adequately answered without addressing the balance of power among the various industry stakeholders. In addition, the exit barriers of existing competitors and the entry barriers of potential new companies need to be analyzed.

Is the pharmaceutical business a profitable place to be in? Given the historically high return-on-equity ratios (around 27% in mid-2003) and net profit margins (around 21% in mid-2003) of pharmaceutical companies, one might suppose that the industry is characterized by little competition and safe and predictable environments.

A method that is often used to analyze industry attractiveness and identify opportunities and threats is Michael Porter's five-forces framework (Porter 1985; see Fig. 11). Porter summarized five principal forces that shape competition in an industry: the bargaining power of suppliers and buyers, the risk of entry from potential competitors, the threats of substitute products, and the degree of rivalry among established companies within an industry. A sixth, regulative force has often been added to complement Porter's five forces in industries with a strong influence from regulation bodies. It is particularly true in the pharmaceutical industry.

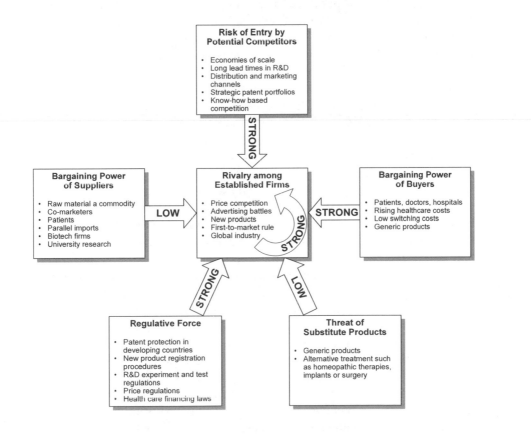

**Fig. 11.** The balance of power in the pharmaceutical industry.

Several opportunities and threats of the pharmaceutical players directly derive from public regulations. This force directly impacts sales, margins, costs of a pharmaceutical business.

## Force 1: Bargaining Power of Suppliers

Suppliers in the pharmaceutical industry include providers of raw materials, biotechnology firms, and manufacturing plants, but also local co-marketing partners or the labor force. Pharmaceutical companies may have different suppliers if they compete in the OTC, ethical or generic businesses.

In the pharmaceutical industry, suppliers do not seem to have strong bargaining power. In clinical research, for instance, the suppliers are patients who participate in clinical trials, the investigators and their research teams who provide the data, and external contractors. An additional threat may emerge from parallel imports from low-price countries (which has triggered heated discussions over the prospects and dangers of adapting prices for life-saving but expensive treatments to developing economies and the possible threat of re-imports from these countries).

However, pharmaceutical companies are increasingly dependent on bio-technology companies and university research. The negotiation power of biotechnology companies has constantly grown over the last years, resulting in pharma-biotech deals that assign up to half of the profits and revenues to the smaller biotech partner today. However, pharmaceutical and biotechnology companies seem to prefer a co-existence rather than direct competition. While biotechnology companies provide early-stage input into the collaborations via new technologies or compounds, the pharmaceutical companies provide their broad and extensive marketing channels and sales force.

In addition, the biotechnology venture capital industry has matured in the past years which made it more difficult to acquire biotechnology start-ups (although some biotechnology companies have started to aggregate and announce their intention to become fully-fledged pharmaceutical companies, e.g., Celera and Axys Pharmaceuticals in 2002). While alliances have thus become an important source of new products and marketing agreements, the overall threat of biotechnology companies on the majority of pharmaceutical companies seems to be fairly moderate. It is generally not expected that biotechnology companies will turn into fully integrated pharmaceutical companies and compete via similar business models.

## Force 2: Bargaining Power of Buyers

> *"We must never forget that innovation is an access issue – access for those with unmet medical needs. We must balance the needs of patients for marketed medicines today with the needs of patients depending on new medicines in the future."*
>
> *Henry A. McKinnell, Jr.,*
> *former President and CEO, Pfizer*

Buyers in the pharmaceutical industry usually include the patients (particularly in the OTC business), medical doctors who prescribe drugs, hospital boards who authorize the purchase of new treatments and drugs or pharmacists optimizing their stock of medication.

However, the ultimate consumer – the patient – usually does not have much influence on a medical doctor's or physician's decision about a certain prescriptive drug, since their knowledge about the respective drug and its consequences tends to be limited. Moreover, the patient normally does not carry the costs of the product. These costs are typically covered by health insurance companies. As a consequence, the consumer/patient was traditionally less likely to develop a sense of cost consciousness regarding the pharmaceutical products being used. Hence, the product's quality usually was almost the only factor that influenced the purchasing decision.

In accordance with a recent change in the national healthcare system, this is expected to change: The patient participates in the costs and, therefore, becomes more price sensitive. Co-payments for branded prescription drugs are a first step towards this direction. Subsequently, the informed patient is increasingly gaining in importance. In the case of non-prescription drugs (i.e., OTC drugs), the patients are usually able to select the drugs themselves. This leads to a higher cost-consciousness on the consumer's side. Health insurance companies are thus increasingly trying to market OTC drugs in order to reduce their reimbursement efforts.

The emergence of self-organized patient groups additionally requires pharmaceutical companies to shift more attention towards direct-to-customer or direct-to-patient marketing strategies. While buyers of pharmaceutical products are still a highly fragmented group, the buying power of large patient groups particularly in the U.S. has risen considerably over the last years. The so-called Health Maintenance Organizations (HMOs) aggregate and represent the interests of multiple patients. They have been very successful in negotiating prices that are favorable to patients. Thus, the buyers can exercise a strong influence over prices, often seeking price reductions for bulk purchases or threatening to switch to other suppliers (particularly in the generics business). The HMO model is particularly applicable in the U.S. where prices of prescription drugs are not subject to price regulation by the government.

Despite of the threat of HMOs, most pharmaceutical companies have been successful at establishing direct marketing relationships with doctors and patients around the world. Large groups of sales representatives and Medical Science Liaisons (MSLs) ensure appropriate awareness among physicians for new and existing products on the market. However, regulatory scrutiny has recently increased which leads the pharmaceutical companies to rethink and reassess their sales strategies. Particularly the high number of doctor visits by sales representatives has caused regulatory authorities to intervene. More focused approaches that deliver information with higher medical value to physicians are likely to represent the sales force model of the future.

The buying power of doctors seems to have increased slightly, and switching costs are relatively low. At the same time, governments and health authorities influence local prices in their attempts to contain healthcare costs. In countries with nationalized healthcare and tight price controls, buyer power is higher: Prescription prices in most European countries are about 30 to 50 percent lower than in the U.S. (Freudenheim and Peterson 2001).

## Force 3: Risk of Entry from Potential Competitors

New entrants are usually faced with the following entry barriers:

- Economies of scale such as in R&D, marketing, and sales;
- Slow success rates in new drug development;
- Image, established relationships, and brand value;
- Capital requirements and financial resources;
- Access to distribution channels;
- Ability and capacity to deal with regulatory agencies and patents.

Even small biotech firms focusing on a single technology must spend hundreds of million of dollars just to propose a potential product. Established pharmaceutical companies have manufacturing and distribution systems that are hard to replicate, a strategic patent portfolio preventing competitors to enter new disease areas, and large marketing budgets to protect their brands. Nevertheless, some companies are trying to enter the pharmaceutical market, such as contract research organizations vertically expanding their businesses.

Furthermore, patent protection does not protect against competition from generic products. While generics capture about 50 percent of unit sales with continuous growth, they are far less profitable though. Pfizer's 2001 prescription drug revenues of US$ 26.3 billion was almost five times the combined sales of the 11 leading generic drug makers covered in Standard & Poor's Industry Survey (Saftlas 2001).

## Force 4: Threat of Substitute Products

Substitute products perform the same function as existing products, or better. Generic products are serious substitutes for original products at a lower price. While generics mount an increasing threat to profitability of large pharmaceutical companies, they might also offer opportunities. Novartis, for example, proactively approached the threat of generics and now has emerged as one of the largest generics companies itself by selling various generic products under the global umbrella name Sandoz.

The worldwide generics market has experienced significant growth in unit sales. However, the market share of generics compared to the total drug market is still comparatively small due to the generic drugs' relatively low prices. A reason might be that manufacturers of generics just concentrate on drugs with a very high sales volume in order to reach a critical mass in sales and margins quickly, thereby ignoring smaller niche markets that might be highly profitable for the pharmaceutical companies.

Besides of generics, some other substitutes for pharmaceutical products might include certain medical devices or alternative therapies. Even hospitalization may be a substitute for drug treatments. For instance, surgery may make drug intervention unnecessary. On a cost-to-value basis, however, surgery, prolonged medical care and hospitalization are less attractive.

In many countries, for instance Germany, new substitute products will be financed by the insurance firms only if the added value of the new product is proven to be much higher than the old product. With such regulations the insurance firms try to reduce costs since new products are typically more expensive than the older one.

Alternative therapies such as homeopathic remedies, acupuncture, and herbal medicines are all still considered medically unproven and are usually not covered by health insurance. But traditional treatment knowledge might change with a new generation of medical doctors who are educated more openly and are trained to consider certain patients' wishes for soft treatments. If these products begin to demonstrate medical efficacy, they will be quickly absorbed to become part of conventional medicine. Overall, the risk of unmanageable exposure to substitute products in the pharmaceutical industry is relatively low. Strongest product substitutes still come from the innovative pharmaceutical companies themselves.

## Force 5: Rivalry among Established Companies

The rivalry is moderately intense since the pharmaceutical industry is still comparatively fragmented. Although the top 20 drug manufacturers control a little less than 60 percent of the market, no single company controls more than a 9 percent share. Competitors try to improve their position in the marketplace by means of price competition, acquisitions, advertising battles and new product introductions. This rivalry is particularly intense in saturated markets (e.g., cardiovascular and central nervous systems, pain relievers), and less intense in growing markets (e.g., oncology or immune disorders).

Most industry profits come from patented products or therapies. The so called 'me-too' products tend to be less profitable. As individual drug therapies tend to be quite focused on particular markets, competition is somewhat limited. Nevertheless, generics are improving their position at the expense of blockbuster drugs going off patent (experiencing price drops of up to 80 percent), and have increased their share of unit volume to 47 percent in 2000, up from 33 percent in 1990 (PhRMA 2001).

Rivalry is typically fought over time-to-market, since first-to-market companies gain a relatively high market share and thus are more likely to recoup R&D and marketing expenses. Global product introductions help achieve market share, and therefore large companies have an edge over smaller companies thanks to more developed marketing and distribution systems.

## Force 6: The Regulators

Public laws and regulations play perhaps a greater role in the pharmaceutical industry than in any other. The regulative force impacts pharmaceutical innovation on several levels: (1) R&D regulations and product registrations, (2) price regulations and national healthcare systems, and (3) intellectual property rights.

(1) R&D regulations in experiments are mainly affected by national product registration agencies, such as the Food and Drug Administration (FDA) in the U.S. or the European Medicines Evaluation Agency (EMEA) in Europe. These governmental agencies stipulate authorization and registration procedures for all new drugs submitted for approval in their respective markets. New drugs must prove that they are suitable for use in human beings and the respective benefit-risk profile has to be determined prior to marketing approval. Only after a medical product has cleared all hurdles – and therefore fulfills regulations regarding quality, efficacy, and safety – is it granted authorization.

The FDA, for example, interferes at two stages during a new drug authorization/registration process. The first comes right after the pre-clinical tests, where the FDA's Center for Drug Evaluation and Research (CDER) determines if the new drug is suitable for use in clinical trials (i.e. in trials with humans). This process is called the Investigational New Drug (IND) Review Process. An IND permission has to be kept active annually by sending, for example, annual reports. In addition, projects are discussed with the FDA frequently, especially before entry into phase III clinical trials and submission. After the clinical tests have been successful, the CDER determines during a second step the benefit-risk profile of a new drug prior to approval for marketing. This process is referred to as the New Drug Application (NDA) Review Process.

In general, a high-quality test on pharmaceuticals is time consuming and expensive. However, the FDA uses timesaving processes to speed up introduction of important new drugs to patients with particular needs. An accelerated approval may be granted to priority drugs that show promise in the treatment of serious and life-threatening diseases for which there is no adequate therapy. Treatment Investigational New Drug designations enable patients not enrolled in the clinical trials to use promising life-saving drugs while they are still in the testing stage. For example, when the first tests of the antiviral drug AZT in 1985 showed encouraging results in 330 AIDS patients, the FDA authorized a Treatment IND for more than 4,000 people with AIDS before AZT was approved for marketing.

The median length of time required to review and approve a new drug varies from 1.1 years in the UK to between 1.4 and 1.7 years in Germany, Australia, Spain, and the USA. In general, it has to be considered that legal regulations most often reflect the entire society's position towards technology. In highly-developed industrial countries, a decline in public acceptance of new technologies, such as bio- and gene-technology, can be observed. Restrictive regulations for experiments on animals and stem cell research are typical examples. Thus, pharmaceutical companies might also consider regulations as a driver for shifting their research abroad. Besides approvals for clinical trials in humans, animal trials and inventions in gene technology are covered by strict authorization processes as well.

(2) In most countries drug prices are regulated by federal authorities (directly or indirectly). The United States and New Zealand are the only two countries in the world that have no federal price regulation for drugs. In some countries the price of a product is fixed according to the social costs of the society. Yet in other countries, the price of a drug is defined by its innovativeness as measured by the number of patents in that area (e.g., in Brazil). However, national healthcare systems always have the primary and most direct impact on product prices, which are reimbursed by health insurance organizations.

(3) The overall purpose of patent law is to support research and ensure that all interests are satisfied. On the one hand, innovations should be made available in the interest of the public. On the other hand, innovators should have an incentive to innovate by being assured that their inventions are protected against unlawful imitation and replication of their knowledge. From a competitive perspective, patents are essential because it is not difficult to ascertain the respective substances of a drug and, consequently copy or imitate pharmaceutical products. Studies have shown that patents are the most effective means of appropriation. 65 percent of pharmaceutical inventions would not have been introduced without patent protection, compared to a cross-industry average of 8 percent (Reuters 2002). Patent protection is unclear in some key areas of pharmaceutical R&D, for instance at the time of writing it is still unclear to what extent genes can be patented (and thus 'owned'). Sometimes, international patent law is only accepted if national interests are maintained. Brazil, for example, threatened over the last ten years several times to suspend domestic compliance with international patent rights for malaria drugs unless certain license fees were dropped.

## Conclusions

The pharmaceutical industry covers a broad range of product groups, from vitamins over fine chemicals, plant protection agents and animal medicine to the traditional pharmaceuticals and biopharmaceuticals. Within the group of pharmaceuticals, there are several different product categories that address multiple different therapeutic areas.

But the high complexity of the industry itself doesn't seem to be biggest hurdle for companies' success. Despite of potentially attractive profit margins and a favorable balance of power with respect to suppliers and product substitutes, the pharmaceutical industry is overall a tough industry to be in. What used to be a safe haven for market leaders increasingly becomes a substitution market. While many diseases still await effective treatment, most of the obvious or easy drug targets have been discovered, and economically viable therapies have been developed. Start-ups and entrants employing new technologies compete with incumbent pharmaceuticals over international markets and new innovations.

While patent protection usually secures a monopolistic market power for a limited time, the threat of generics is immense. Sales of branded products that have been established over years will erode within weeks. Most pharmaceutical companies still don't know how to handle this competitive threat.

# III. The Science and Technology Challenge: How to Find New Drugs

## Rise of the Biotechnology Industry: Boosting Innovation

Due to the enormous costs of building up a pharmaceutical R&D infrastructure, it was generally believed in the late 1970s and early 1980s that no new company would ever be able to enter the pharmaceutical industry and to compete with the industry's giants (see Robbins-Roth 2001). However, some entrepreneurs were not impressed with this challenge and created an entirely new industry – the biotechnology industry. Besides of an innovative management approach as well as creative funding strategies, the main drivers for the rise of the biotechnology industry have been the emergence of new sciences and technologies. While innovation activities of established pharmaceutical companies were traditionally based on organic chemistry, biochemistry and chemical engineering, biotechnology companies have built a reputation in many novel areas, such as cell biology, molecular genetics, protein chemistry and encymology (Whittaker and Bower 1994).

The application of biotechnology in the pharmaceutical industry started with the development of scientific techniques, such as genetic engineering and antibody production. The technique of genetic engineering was developed in 1973, and received its first commercial pharmaceutical application four years later when Eli Lilly started the development of recombinant human insulin in cooperation with Genentech. The resulting product, Humulin, became the first biotechnology product when launched in 1983 (Reuters 2002).

By the end of 2000, a total of 76 biotechnology drugs had been approved for marketing, and 369 biotechnology drugs were in human clinical testing for more than 200 disease targets, accounting for around a third of all medicines in clinical development (Reuters 2002). A total of about 1,500 compounds were in the overall development stage around the year 2000 (Zanetti and Steiner 2001).

Following their launch, these early biotechnology products accounted for an average of 13.4 percent of all pharmaceutical products launched between 1991 and 1995, rising to 18.2 percent of all products launched between 1996 and 2000 (Reuters 2002). The first biotechnology drugs that reach blockbuster status and generated in excess of US$ 1 billion in sales per year were Procrit (Johnson&Johnson), Epogen (Amgen), Neupogen (Amgen), and Humulin (Genentech and Eli Lilly).

However, just one out of 47 biotechnology companies possesses a successful product (see Jakob 2003). Moreover, just 24 of the 3,000 biotechnology companies worldwide were profitable in 2000 (see WGZ Bank 2002).

In 2006, the U.S. is still the leader in this critical industry, and the U.S. still has the lion's share of product sales and income. However, the growth in actual numbers of new company development has been fairly stagnating. The U.S. has maintained the same level in terms of numbers of biotech companies over the last few years with approximately 1,500 firms, compared to about 1,500 in Europe, 1,500 in Asia, and about 450 in Canada. However, the U.S. still has the largest stock markets for biotech companies, but it is beginning to lose ground in biotech initial public offerings as IPOs are taking place in several European countries as well as Israel, India, Australia, and Japan.

While there is still high growth in the formation of new biotechnology companies in the U.S., lots of biotechnology companies also fail or are acquired by larger companies. Biotech is no longer just a U.S. phenomenon. Countries such as Switzerland, China, Israel, Korea, and Japan have been catching up largely over the last years.

Due to the fact that most biotechnology firms have no product on the market yet and, hence, are heavily reliant on their research and development activities, they are of particular interest to established pharmaceutical companies' R&D managers. According to Reuters (2002), the advancement of biotechnology impacts the pharmaceutical value chain in two major ways:

1. As the growth of new biotechnology product launches continues to outpace that of traditional pharmaceutical products, integrated pharmaceutical companies have established significant access to these new technologies through licensing agreements and alliances with biotechnology companies.
2. As the leading biotechnology companies have evolved through the development of key products, they have built up critical mass in the development and marketing functions in order to compete directly with the integrated pharmaceutical companies across the value chain.

According to Recombinant Capital (2005), more than 600 alliances between pharmaceutical and biotechnology firms are formed every year around the world with a deal value of over US$ 30 billion. The nature of these alliances varies: In some instances, a biotechnology shop exchanges an exclusive license to market and sell a patented drug to a pharmaceutical company that is willing to pay some research costs up front. Such agreements may also include limited use of the pharmaceutical company's manufacturing and distribution channels.

Over the recent past, the negotiation power and balance in collaborations between pharmaceutical and biotech companies has clearly shifted in favor of the biotech companies. While it has been usual for biotech firms to receive between 5 to 10 percent of the revenues incurred in mutual projects, this number has grown in some cases to around 50 percent (Zanetti and Steiner 2001). Many young biotech ventures have become so-called 'born globals', small firms with global activities and thus many similar challenges like large firms (Gassmann and Keupp 2007). Some biotech companies have been successfully negotiating for co-promotion and manufacturing rights for current and future products with big pharmaceutical companies. For example, Exclixis (in collaboration with GlaxoSmithKline) retained North-American co-promotion rights for multiple compounds under mutual development, Genta (in collaboration with Aventis) retained U.S. co-promotion and manufacturing rights for the compound Genasense, and Neurocrine (in collaboration with Pfizer) retained U.S. co-promotion rights for its compound Indipplon as well as co-promotion rights to the product Zoloft (Datamonitor 2003).

In some other instances, a pharmaceutical company may make a cash investment in exchange for a portion of future revenues and/or an equity stake in the biotechnology partner. This type of relationship is often tied to a marketing and distribution deal like the one described above. As a result, it is not unusual for a large pharmaceutical company to have biotechnology holdings that give them a substantial piece of the action. For example, Roche owns a majority stake in the biotech firm Genentech and sources lots of compounds into its pipeline. Novartis used to own a substantial equity stake in the biotech firm Chiron and only recently acquired the firm's remaining shares.

Research on alliances between biotechnology and pharmaceutical firms suggests that alliances are becoming more sophisticated and mature, that drug companies are poles of the alliance networks, and that new biotechnology firms play a mediating role in transforming scientific knowledge into patented technologies (see Lin 2001). A prominent example of a successful European biotechnology firm the Swiss company Cytos Biotechnology.

**Cytos Biotechnology: Innovation made in Switzerland**

Founded in 1995 as a spin-off of the Swiss Federal Institute of Technology (ETH) in Zurich, Cytos became a publicly listed biotechnology company in October 2002. Today, in 2007, Cytos employs around 130 people. Cytos' CEO, Dr. Wolfgang Renner, won the Swiss Entrepreneur-of-the-Year Award in 2000.

The scientific foundation for Cytos' strategy is the product-platform concept. Cytos applies its integrated technology platform across a broad range of disease areas to maximize opportunities for product development and to build a versatile portfolio of novel therapeutic molecules.

Cytos' core competencies revolve around working with proteins. Cytos' Immunodrugs™ represent a new class of biopharmaceuticals that are designed to instruct the patient's immune system to produce a desired therapeutic antibody or cytotoxic T cell response to reverse or prevent disease progression. When originated, this approach represented a paradigm shift away from passive immunization towards an active immunization of the patient against a disease-related protein and combines the hallmarks of classical pharmacology with vaccination.

As of April 2007, Cytos had 22 projects in its R&D pipeline, most of them in pre-clinical stages. Cytos is partnering with Novartis on two projects, one Phase II project in the respiratory space as well as another Phase I project targeting Alzheimer's disease.

Due to increased competition from biotechnology companies which are forced to using the latest drug discovery techniques in order to survive in the market, every pharmaceutical company is facing the pressure to be among the technological leaders in their respective area. The following paradigm shift was observed in the past: Traditional approaches and sequential experimentation in drug discovery have increasingly been complemented by automated, mass-production analyses of compound libraries and computer-based experimentation using several different new technologies. In addition, the discovery of the Human Genome is expected to further supplement this paradigm shift in pharmaceutical R&D. While more than 500 biological targets for drugs have been identified so far, it is estimated that the Human Genome Project will produce another 3,000 to 10,000 new targets (Pfeiffer 2000).

The application of new sciences and technologies will lead to the following essential changes and impacts on the drug discovery process (see also Nightingale 2000):

- The nature of scientific understanding of diseases becomes more fundamental. A more detailed understanding of drug target function in the context of a molecular mode of disease onset, progression and chronicity will increase the quality of applied targets;
- The scale of experimentation undergoes fundamental changes and shifts from an individual initiative to an automated mass-production process;
- The cycles of trial and error experimentation are complemented by computer simulations;
- Complementary screening is performed by computer simulations;
- Single compounds are replaced by compound libraries;
- Structural complexity and diversity of compound libraries will increase.

This chapter focuses on new sciences and technologies as the underlying drivers for innovation in the pharmaceutical industry (see Fig. 12). They

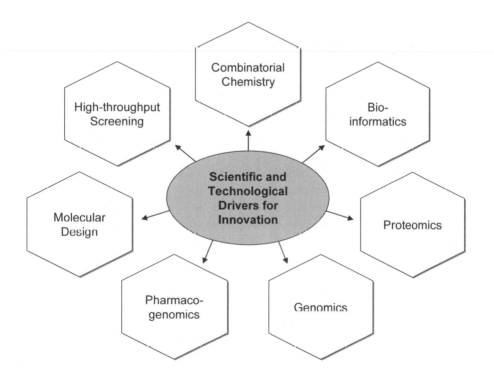

**Fig. 12.** New sciences and technologies as drivers for innovation.

enable the different parts of pharmaceutical research and development and lead to significant and revolutionizing results in pharmaceutical innovation.

As R&D costs can escalate dramatically in the later phases of the R&D process (e.g., up to 80 percent of total R&D expenditures might incur during the clinical trials), the impact of new scientific and technological input is expected to be the highest in the very early stages of research and discovery.

## High-Throughput Screening: Fail Earlier, Succeed Sooner

High-throughput screening (HTS) or ultra high-throughput screening (UHTS) belong to a wide range of novel drug discovery technologies, which are revolutionizing pharmaceutical research.

„These new plate formats have arisen as a potential answer to the problematic question being asked at most major pharmaceutical companies: How can we screen more targets and more samples cheaply?" (Houston and Banks 1997).

The consistent application of novel drug discovery technologies allows for the automation of much of the discovery function, promoting a more comprehensive and consistent screening process. Both the quality and quantity of resultant lead compounds are expected to increase. The overall goal of improving the early phase in drug discovery is to identify promising chemical samples or entities as soon as possible. The guideline here is to ‚fail earlier in order to succeed sooner'.

In the 1990s, high-throughput screening became the major tool for lead identification. HTS is the biological technology that allows large numbers of chemicals to be automatically tested for their impact on biological activity, representing components of disease. It comprises of a system for data handling, an array of compounds to be tested, a robot to perform the testing and a biological test configured for automation.

As a result, the yearly throughput of a typical lead discovery group increased from about 75,000 samples tested on about 20 targets to over a million samples tested on over 100 targets (Houston and Banks 1997). Today, UHTS allows for simultaneously screening of more than 100,000 substances per day in a fully automated way. Some companies achieved improvements in screening effectiveness well above a multiple of 25 by using HTS and UHTS technologies (see Reuters 2002).

While the quantity of screened substances is increasing tremendously, the screening technologies, however, do not have an impact on the quality of the outcome. Besides screening through a vast number of substances, it is therefore equally important to have the right substances included in the pool of all substances that are to be screened.

## Combinatorial Chemistry: Cut Experimental Cycle Times

Along with high-throughput screening, combinatorial chemistry is considered to be one of the most essential tools for drug discovery. The two technology platforms of combinatorial chemistry and HTS account for more than half of all spending on new discovery technologies in the pharmaceutical industry (Reuters 2002).

The emergence of combinatorial chemistry was triggered by the increasing application of HTS technologies. With the surge of high-throughput screening technologies, a bottleneck in the discovery process occurred as the production of compounds did not expand at the same rate. With a shift from being able to screen hundreds of compounds to being able to screen tens-of-thousands of compounds in the early 1990s, it became obvious that pharmaceutical firms could test all their compounds very quickly. Hence, improvements in screening technologies increased demand for compounds and created a 'reverse salient' in synthetic chemistry (Nightingale 2000). A new technology had to fill this vacuum.

Combinatorial chemistry is a technology that allows large numbers of compounds to be made by the systemic and repetitive covalent connection of a set of different 'building blocks' of varying structures to each other. This helped pharmaceutical research be able to yield a large array of diverse molecular entities. Hence, combinatorial chemistry is a mass-production technology that synthesizes large numbers of compounds in parallel.

When widely introduced in the 1990s, combinatorial chemistry was able to reduce experimental cycle times by more than eight hundred times and lowered costs and risks by more than six hundred times compared to traditional methods (Booz Allen & Hamilton 1997).

While HTS and combinatorial chemistry are definitely major improvements in pharmaceutical research, these technologies remain relatively novel and their transition into launched products is yet to be seen. It is not surprising that many experts today still believe that serendipity is a key success factor.

## Bioinformatics: More than 100 Gigabytes of Data per Day

*"You have 50,000 to 100,000 genes in the body, and each cell expresses a subset of those genes. We take the RNA from those cells and make copies, called cDNA. Those copies are put into what we call expression plasmids and then put into bacteria, so we have hundreds of thousands of these bacteria all with one specific cDNA sequence to form what is called a 'library' of cDNA clones."*

*Raymond Goodwin,*
*2001 Winner of the PhRMA Discoverers Award*

Bioinformatics generally deals with the acceleration of lead discovery by providing structural data, information and knowledge. The worldwide amount of knowledge doubles every seven years (Davis and Botkin 1994). The number of scientific journals was 100 at the beginning of the 19th century, 1,000 around 1850, over 10,000 in 1900; by 2000 there were around 100,000 worldwide. Today, over 5 million people work in the area of knowledge production in R&D departments – approximately 90 percent of all scientists who have ever lived (Nefiodow 1990; Pfiffner and Stadelmann 1995). Pharmaceutical research is among the leaders in knowledge production. Drivers for the increasing knowledge accumulation include the escalating usage of novel drug discovery technologies as well as external knowledge acquisition.

New technologies in drug discovery produce huge amounts of valuable data and information, which have to be processed and prepared in order to be accessed during the pharmaceutical innovation process. New methods and technologies are necessary to make use of this knowledge. Given that a single pharmaceutical lab can generate more than 100 GB of data per day, this job can only be done by sophisticated information technologies.

In addition, research is increasingly conducted externally. For example, Merck stated in its 2000 annual report that its own research accounts for only 1 percent of the biomedical research in the world. In order to tap into the remaining 99 percent, the company has to actively reach out to universities, research institutions and companies on a global scale to bring the best of technology and potential products into Merck. Toward that end, Merck has now challenged its internal scientists with a new task: to create a virtual lab in their research area. This means that Merck scientists do not just create excellent science in their own lab; instead, they identify and build connections to excellent science in other labs, wherever these labs may be (see Chesbrough 2003). Hence, efficient knowledge acquisition and effective integration in the scientific community becomes increasingly important. Even small start-up companies operate relatively globally in R&D: They acquire their knowledge through cooperation with other complementary companies as well as through public databases (e.g., Internet).

Consequently, information technologies in pharmaceutical research have to deal with both the management of data and knowledge within the corporate boundaries as well as the linkages to the outside research community. Baumann (2003) summarizes the major tasks of information technologies in pharmaceutical R&D as follows:

- To provide and manage databases for the tremendous amount of information;
- To allow the generation of compound profiles for improved target identification and screening;
- To manage genome and protein sequences;
- To visualize 3D data;
- To collect data on model organisms;
- To manage the huge amount of data from the clinical tests and provide feedback to the early phases of drug discovery;
- To enable accessibility and sharing of knowledge within the corporation as well as to outside collaborators.

One of the foremost tasks of information technologies in pharmaceutical research is to handle the large amounts of complex data generated throughout all phases of the R&D process. Recent improvements have been seen in data management software, statistical analysis software and the visualization technologies required to illustrate and represent the bulk of data. In the past, computer programs dealt only with single molecules and/or compounds. Today – by having compound libraries – it is possible to compare and explore patterns within the collections of compounds. Compound libraries can also be tested against counterscreens by using statistical techniques to understand why a molecule is selective for a particular substrate. Hence, data is stored and used to help re-analyze new data. This allows a more detailed understanding of the structure-activity relationship (see also Nightingale 2000). The comprehensive and complex databases also allow determining the value of purchasing compounds. Clinical trial design can also be improved through a superior understanding of how a drug is likely to act.

The Internet will emerge as a key tool and will provide pharmaceutical companies with the ability to more effectively interact with partners, regulators and consumers. Internet-based technologies hold the potential to impact every stage of the pharmaceutical value chain. The ability to access and share data, and to interact and communicate within and across organizations, will determine how successfully new technologies are integrated. Investment in Internet technologies should realize significant productivity gains across the research and the development functions.

A survey among R&D executives conducted by Accenture showed that 54 percent of respondents agreed that new Internet technologies are fundamentally changing R&D processes (Accenture 2001b). 86 percent believed these technologies would have a great impact in the near future, while 58 percent said that there is already a high level of urgency within their organizations to adopt new technologies. However, barriers to the adoption of new Internet technologies included concerns over the security of company proprietary information, regulatory concerns about patient confidentiality, and budget and staffing issues.

In summary, bioinformatics is expected to lead to very valuable improvements in the early stages of pharmaceutical research. By using increasingly sophisticated information technologies in the early phase, economies of scale therefore become less important.

## Proteomics: Profiting from the Human Genome Project

The term proteome refers to all the proteins expressed by a genome, and proteomics is dealing with proteins produced by cells and organisms. The approximately 30,000 genes defined by the Human Genome Project translate into 300,000 to 1 million proteins when alternate splicing and post-translational modifications are considered. While a genome remains unchanged to a large extent, the proteins in any particular cell change dramatically as genes are turned on and off in response to its environment.

Most drugs work on proteins or protein receptors. Hence, a primary challenge of proteomics is to identify differences between the pattern of a healthy and a sick person, compare them, and identify and isolate the guilty proteins. Consequently, proteomics covers efforts to obtain complete descriptions of the gene products in a cell or organism. Today, proteomics includes not only the identification and quantification of proteins, but also the determination of their localization, modifications, interactions, activities, and, ultimately, their function.

It is generally believed that through proteomics new disease markers and drug targets can be identified that will help design drugs for the prevention, diagnosis as well as treatment of diseases. While the future of biotechnology and medicine will be impacted greatly by proteomics, there is much yet to do to realize the potential benefits.

Several difficulties arise when studying proteins. Proteins are more difficult to work with than DNA and RNA. Proteins cannot be amplified like DNA, therefore less abundant sequences are more difficult to detect. Proteins have secondary and tertiary structures that must often be maintained during their analysis. Proteins can be denatured by the action of enzymes, heat, light or by the impact of physical forces. Some proteins are difficult to analyze due to their poor solubility.

As protein identification and characterization technologies are improving, the bottleneck in proteomics will be shifting from generating proteomic information to applying it.

## Genomics: Towards Individualization and Mass Customization

> *"As the genomic revolution continues, we will invent medicines we could not even envision just a few years ago."*
>
> *Henry A. McKinnell, Jr.,*
> *former President and CEO, Pfizer*

Genomics describes the process of identifying genes involved in diseases through the comparison of the genomes of individuals with and without disease. Genomics is the most high profile of the many enabling technologies recently developed in pharmaceutical R&D. It has been heralded as having the potential to revolutionize both medicine and the entire pharmaceutical industry. Genomic technologies will enable the identification of 3,000 to 10,000 new drug targets, compared with the current number of 500 (Pfeiffer 2000). The integration of genomics and other technologies will lead to a shift from broadly targeted drugs to more focused medicines with much higher therapeutic value for the target population. Genomics is the pharmaceutical answer to mass customization: Realizing economies of scale with individualized drugs.

While genomic technologies allow for a better understanding of drug target function in genomic population subsets, or even individuals, it raises great commercial and financial concerns. The time and resources that must be spent to develop genetic profiles and market sizes for tailored drugs are much smaller, resulting in the need for completely different portfolio management strategies. Exploiting this opportunity will require that companies leverage genotype-based diagnostics into personalized medicine, completely shifting the end-game equation from high-volume/high-value (e.g., blockbuster drugs) to small-volume/higher-value (individualized) drugs. While some believe that personalized medicine will be of limited importance, others are convinced that it will have a broad impact in the industry and further, that using genotype-based elimination/exclusion of major side effects will actually create even larger blockbuster products than is possible based upon today's approach in developing and prescribing medicines (Accenture 2001a).

New genomic biology has accelerated the process of discovering novel targets, but a certain lack of maturity still characterizes technologies such as functional genomics, which play critical roles in determining the biological functions of targets, and in translating knowledge into drugs. Validation of the many targets generated by genomic methods is the major bottleneck in drug discovery together with the structural complexity and diversity of screenable compounds.

The use of genomics beyond target generation has generated great interest, but there is no clear picture yet as to how to best utilize genetics for value creation. According to research by Reuters (2002), the application of disease genetics and pharmacogenetics together could, in the very best case, save as much as two-thirds on the current cost to develop a drug.

The genomic revolution began in 1993 when Human Genome Sciences formed its partnership with SmithKline Beecham. However, it was not until the completion of the first draft of the human genome was announced in 2000 that the accompanying media and investor attention suggested that genomics had become an essential investment for achieving effective drug discovery in the future. No major pharmaceutical company is now without genomics capabilities, whether in-house or accessed through licensing agreements.

For certain organizations, external sourcing of genomics capabilities is a viable long-term strategy. Many drug companies are establishing numerous alliances with genomics focused players to complement their internal capabilities.

Most genomics companies do not usually provide full disclosure of their R&D pipelines. Hence, it is very difficult to assess the current impact of genomics on the pharmaceutical industry. In addition, some very high profile companies, including Incyte and Myriad, do not publish details of the success of their collaborations in terms of generating leads. Similarly, pharmaceutical companies with extensive in-house genomics expertise, such as Novartis and GSK, do not publish details of their early stage research.

Over 2,500 new targets have been discovered by genomics companies by 2001, assuming no duplication. With a minimum of 49 products in preclinical development and at least 13 already in clinical trials, the productivity of the genomics industry seems to be strong (Reuters 2002).

Lehman Bros. estimated that it requires a US$ 100 million annual investment to participate in the genomics arena. To compete in the more aggressive game of an emerging technology, a company might require up to US$ 300 million annually (Agarwal et al. 2001). With an average integrated pharmaceutical company spending around 25 percent of R&D on discovery, an aggressive investment in new technologies would consume more than 75 percent of a middle-tier company such as Roche or Schering-Plough's discovery budget, and would still consume 30 percent of a top-tier company's budget such as GlaxoSmithKline or Pfizer (Reuters 2002).

At the time of writing, the returns on investment of genomic activities are still uncertain. Tremendous uncertainty about the eventual 'best play' scenario in the genomics environment acts as a 'leveler' between the established integrated pharmaceutical companies and the emerging genomics-based companies. The intellectual capital advantage of the highly specialized genomics-based companies may provide them with distinct advantages over larger integrated companies.

The genomic revolution impacts the pharmaceutical value chain in three ways: First, the upside potential of genomics has led to an intensified wave of investment by the integrated pharmaceutical companies, resulting in increased licensing agreements and alliances with genomics-based companies. Second, the level of investment required to fully integrate genomics knowledge and technologies extends competitive advantages for the top-tier global pharmaceutical companies through their ability to access capital. Third, uncertainty over the eventual impact of genomics is creating something of a level playing field for future competition within the pharmaceutical industry. The eventual costs and benefits could help towards redistributing the balance of power between the integrated pharmaceutical and the specialized genomics-based companies (Reuters 2002).

## Pharmacogenomics: Create Tailor-made Drugs

Pharmacogenomics describes how an individual's genetic inheritance affects the body's response to drugs. Pharmacogenomics combines traditional pharmaceutical sciences such as biochemistry with annotated knowledge of genes, proteins, and single nucleotide polymorphisms. The term is derived from the words pharmacology and genomics and is thus at the intersection of pharmaceuticals and genetics. Hence, pharmacogenomics is a discipline that primarily deals with the production of tailor-made drugs for individuals. The drugs are then expected to be adapted to each person's own genetic makeup. Environment, diet, age, lifestyle, and health all can influence a person's response to medicines, but understanding an individual's genetic makeup is thought to be the key to creating personalized drugs with greater efficacy and safety.

Currently, physicians prescribe medication through a trial-and-error method of matching patients with the right drugs. If the prescribed medication does not work for the patient the first time, the physician will try a different drug or dosage, repeating the process until the patient improves. As pharmacogenomics becomes more advanced, physicians eventually will be able to prescribe medication based on an individual patient's genotype, maximizing effectiveness while minimizing side effects.

In discovery, pharmacogenomics may facilitate targeting, understanding of disease pathways, and design of interventions for diseases with multiple genetic etiologies (e.g., breast cancer); along with variants of the same gene in a disease pathway. Differences in genes can also impact drug kinetics, (i.e., absorption, distribution, metabolism and elimination). In development, pharmacogenomics may improve the success rate of clinical trials through use of patient subsets with specific genetic risks and reduced chances of toxicities and side effects (Accenture 2001a).

Once pharmacogenomics provides tailored drug therapy based on genetically determined variation in effectiveness and side effects, the major benefits could be as follows:

- More powerful medicines;
- Better, safer drugs the first time;
- More accurate methods of determining appropriate drug dosages;
- Advanced screening for disease;
- Better vaccines;
- Improvements in the drug discovery and approval process.

Finally, pharmacogenomics is expected to lead to an overall decrease in the cost of healthcare due to decreases in:

- The number of adverse drug reactions;
- The number of failed drug trials;
- The time it takes to get a drug approved;
- The length of time patients are on medication;
- The number of medications patients take to find an effective therapy;
- The effects of a disease on the body (through early detection).

## Molecular Design: From Experimenting to Analytic Design

While the targets of most drugs are proteins, the molecular design of drugs – also referred to as rational design – tries to discover new drugs by looking at the structure of the underlying proteins. By contrast, most other new drug discovery technologies, such as high-throughput screening or combinatorial chemistry, rely upon screening through vast inventories of naturally occurring and man-made chemicals, in search of previously undiscovered substances with the desired biological activity. Lead-optimization is mostly achieved by random exploration of the chemical structure through the synthesis of large numbers of chemical derivatives. While this approach has already tremendously improved the pace of drug discovery, many important therapeutic needs remain for which screening-based research has failed to yield acceptably safe and effective drugs.

While all of the novel screening methods are trying to find the relevant substances by eliminating the irrelevant substances, molecular drug design is analytically deriving the design of the target molecules. The latter approach seems to be far more effective and efficient than screening methods because it is based on an analytical process rather than serendipity.

The basic rationale of how almost all drugs work is well known: Nearly every drug works through an interaction with the target molecule or protein, which causes the respective disease. The drug molecule inserts itself into a functionally important crevice of the target protein, like a key in a lock. The drug molecule is then connected to the target and either induces or, more commonly, inhibits the protein's normal function.

Consequently, a better and more direct understanding of the drug-target interaction would make screening through hundreds of thousands of substances obsolete. If it is possible to identify, in advance, the appropriate target for a given therapeutic need including the structure of the target protein, the structure of an ideal drug molecule could easily be designed to interact with the respective target.

Hence, molecular design is involved in exploiting three-dimensional structures of molecular targets as well as the respective drug molecules. X-ray crystallography in conjunction with genetic engineering techniques are typically used to identify, purify, and modify appropriate proteins. High-speed computers with sophisticated software tools are needed, which permit chemists to predict and simulate molecular structure, dynamics and energetics.

After determining the three-dimensional atomic architecture of the target protein and its functionally critical regions, a variety of specialized programs on interactive graphics workstations come into play. A design team develops and evaluates ideas for structures of drug molecules that complement the unique structure and electronic environment of the target protein. The medicinal chemists then chemically synthesize the most promising candidate structures. As in conventional drug discovery strategies, biochemists measure the ability of these newly synthesized drug candidates in order to produce the intended effect upon the target protein. Crystallographers then re-determine the structure of the protein target – now in combination with the candidate drug molecules. They see the detailed structural interactions actually achieved by the candidate drugs with their target. The scientists relate the performance of such compounds measured by familiar biochemical techniques to its structural interactions with the target as revealed by crystallography. The design team then incorporates the results of this analysis into its next generation of compounds.

The drug design methodology consists of iterative cycles of design, simulation, synthesis, structural assessment, and redesign. The pharmaceutical industry tries to adapt design rules known from the machinery industry to the far more complex world of molecules.

## Conclusions

Since its establishment, the pharmaceutical industry has always been one of the most research-intensive and innovative sectors of manufacturing. The most recent scientific and technological revolution in the pharmaceutical industry initially started in the late 1970s and early 1980s with the rise of the biotechnology industry. By now, ever more complex sciences and technologies meant to discover lead substances are being used in pharmaceutical R&D, such as high-throughput screening, combinatorial chemistry, genomics-based technologies, proteomics or rational drug design. The novelty, complexity and strategic impact of these sciences and technologies on the industry and society have led to the general opinion that a new third industrial revolution has begun.

Due to the high complexity of these novel sciences and technologies, no single pharmaceutical company alone will be able to cope with the challenges imposed by these developments. The increasing pressure to gain access to these technologies forces pharmaceutical companies to open their boundaries and look beyond their own research borders. The case of Merck, which claims to contribute only about 1 percent of worldwide biomedical research and is looking for ways to access the remaining 99 percent, is just one example that illustrates what the future landscape in pharmaceutical R&D will look like: Collaborations with universities, research institutions, biotechnology and genomics-based companies will continue to increase. Only the pharmaceutical companies that are able to manage these cooperations optimally will most likely be capable to introduce innovative products successfully to the market.

# IV. The Pipeline Management Challenge: How to Organize Innovation

*"Pharmaceutical companies can best create value by finding a flow of innovative medicines that answer the needs of doctors and their patients. The companies that will succeed in the long term are the ones that best sustain this flow."*

Fred Hassan,
Chairman, CEO and President, Schering-Plough

## The Relevance of Pipeline Management

Today, more than 2,300 drug candidates are currently in clinical trials or at the FDA for review (PhRMA 2007). By far, the most drugs in the pipelines of pharmaceutical and biotechnology companies target the therapeutic area of oncology which covers all types of cancer related diseases. Cardiovascular, central nervous system and respiratory related diseases are other important therapy areas. Depending on the size of their current business, pharmaceutical companies are required to deliver between two and four new drugs every year in order to maintain or exceed the double-digit growth expectations. Given the high attrition rates in drug development, they have to fill the R&D pipeline with as many new drug candidates as possible.

The pharmaceutical industry, however, is suffering from a lack of genuine innovation (Reuters 2003a). In many cases, pharmaceutical companies rely more on patent protection of existing drugs than on the invention of new drugs. Ironically, over-reliance on patents (intended to encourage investment in innovation) is reducing R&D productivity by diverting attention towards protecting existing product revenues from generic competition. This is a successful short-term strategy, given the relatively low costs of post-patent expiration competition vis-à-vis the huge investments required to develop a new molecular entity. But patent defense generates only incremental revenue compared to the potentially huge gains from new innovative products, and it creates an over-reliance on in-licensing to fill long-term revenue gaps.

Relying on blockbusters to drive the required sales growth, irrespective of company size, is an accepted practice provided there is sufficient depth in the pipeline to continually replace revenues lost to generic competition. However, historical analysis of the blockbuster market in 2000 by Reuters (2003a) suggests that this growth strategy has its weaknesses (see page 6). As mentioned earlier, the revenue forecast of year 2000 blockbuster drugs through to 2008 indicated that there will be an overall 3.8 percent decline in blockbuster sales over this period. Hence, companies can no longer simply rely on blockbuster products alone to drive double-digit revenue growth.

Pharmaceutical companies will have to compensate for declining blockbuster growth by other means. In a first step, however, they have started to raise the investor community's attention to this trend. GlaxoSmithKline and Novartis have issued warnings not to underestimate the significance of declining blockbuster sales, given that the industry suffers from weak late-stage pipelines and new chemical entities have become increasingly difficult to find.

However, sustaining the sales and, ideally, sales growth of blockbuster drugs throughout the lifecycle is necessary to optimize returns on R&D investment, and, in the absence of new products with blockbuster potential in the late stage pipeline, to fill gaps in a company's revenue stream.

The commercial strategy traditionally favored by large pharmaceutical companies – reflecting the belief that 'large markets equate to large revenues' – seems to have changed. Some biotechnology companies successfully pursue a different development strategy and target niche indications. What was generally considered an inefficient and low profit strategy may have turned into a high revenue strategy. Amgen's blockbuster Epogen, primarily used to treat anemia associated with renal disease, has proven that an ability to address a high level of unmet need in a single prominent secondary clinical complication can offer significant growth opportunities.

The major threats that all drugs on the market face as they transfer from the growth into the maturity and decline phases of their lifecycles include:

- The introduction of next generation products offering improved clinical efficacy and less side effects (i.e. a better toxicity profile);
- The entrance of competitively priced newer products offering similar clinical benefits;
- The launch of generic competition following patent expiry.

Different strategies exist that allow pharmaceutical companies to protect their drugs on the market. For example, popularity over a prolonged period of time can be maintained by continuously improving a product through reformulations and line extensions. Furthermore, the continued high investment in drug promotion could be another approach to extend revenue streams.

In addition, the emergence of new drug discovery technologies, such as genomics, pharmacogenomics and proteomics, has heralded new opportunities for the pharmaceutical industry to generate products of higher and more selective efficacy. Given the prospective individualization and mass customization in the pharmaceutical industry, concern arises that the era of blockbuster drugs has come to an end. R&D investment is increasingly focused on using genomics and its associated technologies to target smaller patient populations with specific genotypes and, therefore, inherent tendencies towards certain medical conditions. Hence, it is justified to ask whether the mass application of a single drug to a large patient population will remain a viable strategy for the future.

However, there is an emerging belief that pharmacogenomics-derived products will not mean the end of the blockbuster paradigm; rather, they will help change the accepted definition of these high earning products to that of 'multi-busters', a series of personalized therapies that are able to dominate a certain targeted disease area. According to Reuters (2003a), these products will not present a threat to the blockbuster market because:

- Current blockbusters successfully treating a broad range of patients will not be targeted by post-genomic technologies unless they can sustain a product's market presence in the face of increasing competition.
- Post-genomic technologies will enable companies to build disease market franchises that address the different genotype profiles within target patient groups.
- Pharmaceutical companies will pursue a dual strategy of genomics-based diagnostic/therapeutic disease management. This will lower overall costs of future healthcare and justify higher drug prices.

A very good example of a currently marketed drug that illustrates how markets may become micro-segmented under a genomics-driven business model is Novartis' Gleevec. Unlike mass-market megadrugs, Gleevec only targets a small group of patients and medical specialists in the broad therapeutic area of oncology. The following case example illustrates the history and emergence of Gleevec including the story behind how Novartis realized the importance of this specialized niche indication (see also Reuters 2003a).

**Novartis' Gleevec: How genomics-based drugs can target micro-segmented markets**

On 10 May 2001, Gleevec received FDA approval for the treatment of patients with chronic myelogenous leukemia (CML). By then, Gleevec had already become a market leader for the treatment of CML primarily because of its ability to target a chromosomal abnormality that occurs in only a small segment of the population. Gleevec has generated lucrative revenues since its launch in 2001, and achieved revenues of more than US$ 2.5 billion in 2006. This made Gleevec not only the third most successful pharmaceutical launch in 2001 overall, but also one of Novartis' most successful drugs ever. Today, Gleevec is one of the main revenue drivers in Novartis' product portfolio.

Historically, chronic leukemia has not been the focus of significant R&D investment because of the disease's prominence among the frail elderly who cannot tolerate chemotherapy, and because of its relatively low incidence and prevalence. The market for drugs launched for this indication was not considered sufficient in size to allow companies to recoup their R&D investment. Accordingly, only a handful of drugs have been approved for chronic leukemia in the last decade, the majority of which had originally been developed for other indications or rapidly acquired additional, more-lucrative indications following launch.

Gleevec's success partly reflects Novartis' aggressive, pre-launch PR strategy to drive rapid sales growth in an emerging market. Novartis successfully exploited the Internet to generate extensive pre-launch awareness of Gleevec and its benefits among patients, which ultimately led to a large surge in demand for the drug immediately upon launch. While Gleevec was still in early phase clinical trials, a U.S. patient became so excited about the drug's trial results that she convinced more than 3,000 other patients and care givers to sign a letter to Novartis' CEO requesting that clinical trials be accelerated. Global 'e-word-of-mouth' spread quickly and Novartis had to mobilize consumer targeted PR to respond to patients' concerns. In the end, during the launch of Gleevec, Novartis' sales representatives were surprised to find leukemia patients in their training rooms who had been cured by Gleevec. These patients told the sales reps their personal stories about how Gleevec saved their lives.

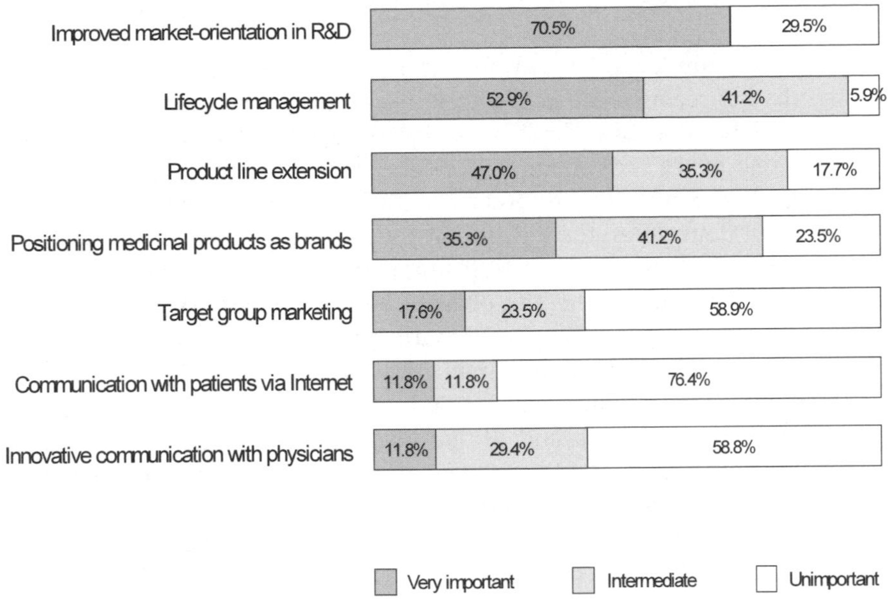

Source: Homburg & Partner (2001)

**Fig. 13.** Major marketing tasks for pharmaceutical companies.

Reflecting that Gleevec's success – besides of its therapeutic value – has mainly been driven by creating awareness in the market, it is not surprising that a survey conducted by Homburg & Partner in collaboration with the University of Mannheim revealed that a market-orientation in pharmaceutical R&D is the foremost marketing task in the pharmaceutical industry going forward (Fig. 13). However, the work of scientists today forms the basis for the industry in 20 years from now. Thus, the length of the innovation cycle makes it very difficult to gain the scientists' interest in today's commercial situation.

The same study by Homburg & Partner (2001) determined that the main driver for an improved customer-orientation is the increasing demand for information by the end-customers. The patients are requesting to become an equal partner in the entire health dialogue. Hence, a shift from a product- to a patient-driven strategy is necessary. This requires a deep understanding of the R&D process and its inherent complexity. The complexity of the pharmaceutical R&D process is discussed in greater detail in the following chapter.

## Complexity and Phases of the R&D Process

While innovation coupled with innovative approaches to bring new drugs to the market seems to be at the core of success in the pharmaceutical industry, it has to be considered that pharmaceutical research and development is one of the most complex endeavors in R&D management in any industry. A research study by Reuters (2002) applied an 'innovation index' to different companies from different industries in order to analyze their relative effectiveness in delivering innovation. A cross-industry comparison allowed benchmarking the pharmaceutical industry against other industries. According to this benchmark, the pharmaceutical industry is ranked worldwide as only the sixth most effective industry in generating innovation, behind aerospace and defense, automotive, electrical/electronics, chemicals and IT hardware. The average pharmaceutical company, however, is almost twice as effective at delivering innovation as the average software and IT services company.

Compared to other industries, the innovation process in the pharmaceutical industry has some very special characteristics, most notably the regulatory environment, which has a direct impact on development time and marketing opportunities, as well as the very high risk during the development. In the past, only 1 of 5,000 product ideas on average was eventually launched on the market, and only 1 out of 10,000 substances used to become a marketable product. However, as new screening technologies are increasingly being used, this ratio has improved significantly. Today, more than 100,000 substances can simultaneously be screened with relatively little effort. Modern information technology has dramatically increased efficiency and effectiveness in the early pharmaceutical innovation phase.

However, only three out of 10 drugs generate revenues that meet or exceed average R&D costs, and 20 percent of products with the highest returns generate 70 percent of total returns (according to a study by Duke University economists cited in Reuters, 2002). While in most industries the decision to terminate a project is made based on economic considerations, the typical reasons in the pharmaceutical industry are primarily scientific or technical.

The average time from initial idea to market is in the region of 13 years. Thus, four out of five researchers retire or move on before they see any commercial impact of their work. This makes incentive systems and motivation a very complicated management issue in pharmaceutical R&D.

Given the obstacles for future R&D performance and productivity, the entire drug discovery process is confronted with structural challenges. Due to the unusually long development period, the effective patent protection

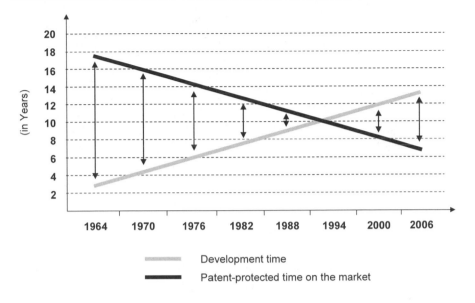

Source: BPI (1999)

**Fig. 14.** The innovation scissors in the pharmaceutical industry.

of a drug in the market is very short. Some countries have therefore extended patent protection for pharmaceutical products by several years. Nevertheless, the trend towards longer development times means an even smaller window to recoup the investments (currently about 7-8 years compared to more then 17 years in the early 1960s). This phenomenon is referred to as the 'innovation scissors' (see Fig. 14).

The primary reason for the long development time is the fact that failures are mostly becoming visible at later stages of the development process (e.g., during the clinical trials). While this pattern significantly extends the average development time, the primary objective for improvements in the drug discovery process should be to "fail earlier" in order to succeed sooner.

The drug discovery process is very complex and includes many different aspects – both managerial and technological – and covers several basic scientific disciplines, such as biology and chemistry (see Fig. 15).

Molecular biology, for example, takes on a particularly important role during the drug discovery process. It contributes to the understanding of the drug target function for onset, progression and chronicity of the disease. The validation of the drug target is key for the quality of lead identification. Hence, molecular biology allows for the development of recom-

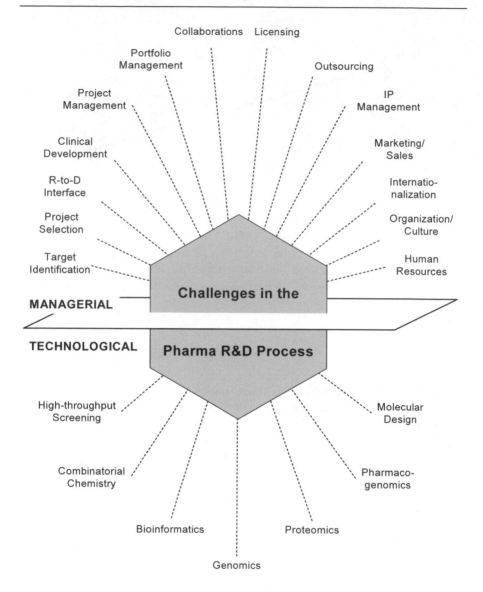

**Fig. 15.** Challenging aspects in the pharmaceutical R&D process.

binant molecules into a new molecular entity using a more rational approach. Mechanistic platforms for multigene-families and signal transduction pathways across disease areas can be established. More complex diseases increasingly require more complex therapeutic concepts and drugs. Sometimes, even a single compound can create its own market.

In chemistry (the primary source of new molecular entities) a shift towards more fundamental science has been observed. Researchers are trying to isolate as many compounds as possible from microorganisms, plants, fungi and marine organisms for new lead identification. The increasing rate of structural complexity can be handled by complementing experiments with computer simulations. Interactions of drug molecules with proteins can be visualized and databases can be used to analyze genes. New database technologies and improved statistical analyses are being used to manage the huge amounts of data.

One single lab can produce more than 100 gigabytes of data per day. Hence, the primary goal in chemistry is to deliver as much input information as possible in order to screen through a sufficient amount of data to discover new substances. Simultaneously and equally important, the quality of the compound collection should be improved. At the beginning of 2003, all drugs on the market only hit in total 120 different targets. The top 100 drugs hit only 43 targets (Zambrowicz and Sands 2003). It is thus very important to screen not only through a large number but also a high quality of data.

Pharmacology is primarily coping with the relevance of the applied disease model. The drug's safety and toxicology is being tested. The major concern is whether the results of the animal trials during the pre-clinical studies are leading to the right products. In addition, the complexity of this task is expected to grow due to the trend towards an increasing segmentation of patients and customization of products to address individual patient profiles.

## The different phases of the R&D process

While the separation of the innovation process into research/pre-project and development phases significantly increases transparency and reduces costs in the main development phase, the introduction of the product into the market is often insufficiently considered. Despite of their different management requirements, many companies do not distinguish between these different phases in R&D projects. For example, Compaq has been making this distinction since 1987. It took a cross-functional team two years to define the specifications for a new personal computer during the pre-project phase. But this extended preparatory work allowed reducing the cost-intensive development phase to nine months.

Highly differentiated phase concepts are commonly accepted and applied in pharmaceutical R&D. The strictly sequential execution of project phases is sometimes considered impractical, but a given sine-qua-non in medical innovation. Projects must be carried out with reviews and milestones, not only to ensure drug candidate quality but also to document good laboratory practice. Only once the drug candidate is approved it is possible for the cost-intensive development phase to use structured engineering methods.

After the spectacular success of the Manhattan and Apollo projects, most companies have concentrated their R&D management efforts on project management. Today we know, at least in principle, how projects work. But we still do not know how to get from the many useful ideas to the vital few projects that an R&D lab is reasonably capable of executing. Even more difficulties arise when the new product is to be introduced to the market. It is therefore suitable to distinguish three phases in the R&D process:

- Pre-project phase: How to create a good product concept and a manageable project
- Development phase: How to manage a project
- Market introduction: How to transfer R&D results efficiently to operations and the customer

The three phases are completely different (see Table 5). Translation of ideas and information is required at each interface. A different language dominates in each phase: the language of science, the language of the company, and the language of the customer. For instance, between the project and the market-introduction phases, we need to translate from the company's technical language to the oftentimes more emotion-based language of the sales force and the customer.

**Table 5.** Differences between pre-project, development, and market introduction phase.

| Criteria | Pre-project Phase | Development Phase | Market Introduction Phase |
|---|---|---|---|
| Budget | Often none / low | Planned / medium | Planned / high |
| Goals | Vague | Detailed | Specified |
| Costs | Low | High | High |
| Processes | Not structured | Structured | Predetermined |
| Results | Unclear | Defined | Negotiated |
| Financial risk | Small | Medium | High |

The three phases differ also from the international viewpoint. The pre-clinical phase can be quite low-key, simmering for years without well-defined structures and strongly dependent on individuals communicating face-to-face to stimulate creativity. The development phase focuses on efficient project execution. Plans and schedules developed in the pre-project phase are carried out, and work packages are allocated like modules to the best-suited teams, wherever they are located in the world. Tight networking exists within the group and efficient coordination at the higher level of project management as well as the inter-group level. Discipline is most important. The third phase of market-introduction is the truly international one: Teams are dispersed all over the world. They belong to different entities, perhaps meeting once a year and maintaining different goals. Negotiating is the name of the game. Tight project management is recommended, but only a few companies successfully apply it.

BASF underscores the distinction between the pre-project and development phases by speaking of R&D 'activities' in the early R&D stages, and R&D 'projects' in later stages. Bayer requires that milestones and project review meetings must not take place before entering the pre-clinical phase

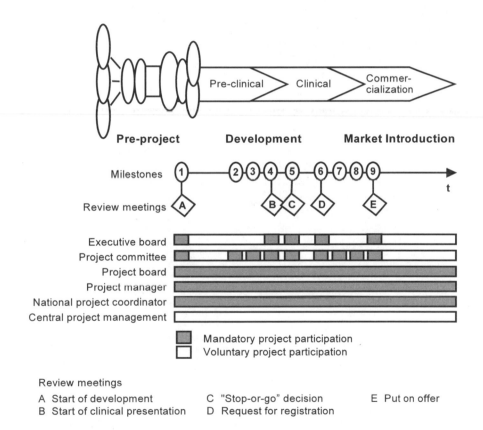

**Fig. 16.** The R&D process at Bayer.

when the project is formally started. Fig. 16 illustrates how Bayer structures its R&D process along pre-project, development and market introduction phase.

Organizationally, companies renowned as innovation leaders in pharmaceutical R&D have typically small, focused research organizations centered on core technologies and therapeutic competencies (Reuters 2002). This approach seems to be the most promising way to deliver effective R&D results.

## The R&D process at Roche

Let us consider the R&D process of Roche to illustrate some of the dynamics and qualities of pharmaceutical innovation (see also Borgulya 2000). The early innovation process is characterized by the research and discovery phase and the pre-clinical trials. During the research stage, the research project is defined and basic research is conducted. The scientists are looking for existing molecules, which could serve as a target for new substances, which are expected to have an impact on the disease which is about to be cured (Fig. 17).

During the screening stage, scientists look for a so-called lead-substance, which influences the target in the desired way. During this

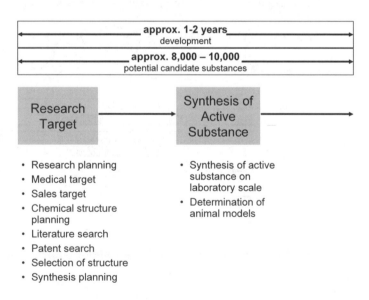

**Fig. 17.** Research concept and discovery of active substance at Roche.

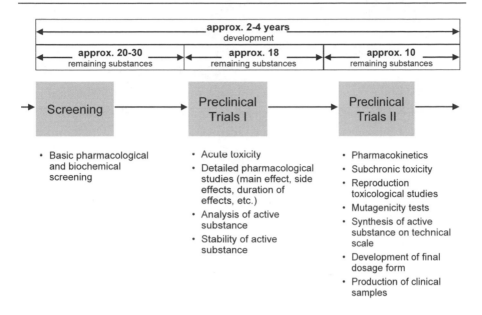

**Fig. 18.** Pre-clinical development at Roche.

stage, almost 90 percent of all potential substances are eliminated due to the lack of desired impacts and/or effects. The remaining substances, which are on average only the few dozen most promising ones, are tested in the pre-clinical trials (Fig. 18). However, due to advancements in computer-based screening technologies, this number might have decreased substantially over the past few years.

Pre-clinical tests try to prove if a new substance takes effect and if it is compliant. The most important issues are to ensure that the new substance is not toxic, does not change genes and does not cause cancer or birth defects. This test-series is usually made using animal experiments. However, the total amount of animal experiments, for example in Switzerland, has decreased dramatically from 2 million in 1983 to less than half a million in 1999. In case the pre-clinical trials are successful, the substance is analyzed regarding its registration for the human being during the clinical trials (Fig. 19).

The clinical trials are separated into three different phases. During phase I, the drug candidate is tested whether its positive animal properties can be extended to humans (compatibility). Between 20 to 80 healthy volunteers are used to determine safety and dosage of the drug candidate. This phase can last up to two years. During phase II, the substance is applied to about

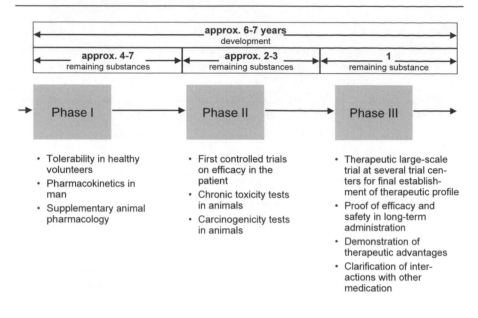

**Fig. 19.** Clinical development at Roche.

100-300 patients as well as to animals. The testing is being done with the intention to find out if the substance is able to cure the disease. During phase III, the substance is tried at a much larger number of patients in order to establish the proper dosage and to determine any adverse reactions to long-term use.

The average number of patients needed for new drug applications has risen from about 1,500 in the late 1970s to about 4,500 in the mid-1990s. Novartis, for instance, included 14,000 patients in the clinical studies of one of their most recent new drugs which was introduced to the market in late 2003. The primary rationale behind this large sample were marketing reasons (i.e. to prove the drug's differentiation from other products). In general, the purpose and the number of patients during the clinical trials may vary significantly depending on the therapeutic area. For example, cancer drugs need entirely different clinical trial sets than drugs against high blood pressure.

If the clinical trials are successful, the new product can be registered with the respective health authorities in each country where the pharmaceutical company intends to launch the drug. After the registration, the new drug can finally be sold on the market accompanied by support from the sales force (see Fig. 20).

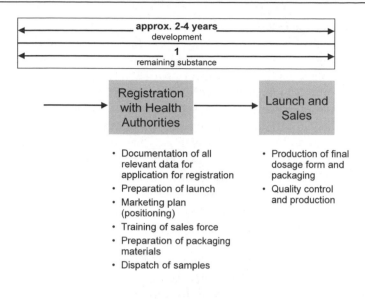

**Fig. 20.** Registration, launch and sales at Roche.

## The Importance of Project and Portfolio Management

As the pharmaceutical R&D process is extremely complex, bringing a new drug from the idea/concept phase to the market introduction phase is a highly difficult endeavor that requires sophisticated project management skills. Moreover, managing multiple projects at the same time represents an even more complex task. The principal objective of portfolio management is to ensure that a well-balanced combination of projects makes use of the company's competencies and is directed at defined therapeutic areas and profitable markets. Access to networks in clinics and market opinion is a key success factor.

Once an overall R&D strategy has been defined, the first step in pharmaceutical project management is to select and evaluate the right projects. Many companies rely on the net-present-value method in order to select projects. This method projects future cash in-flows and out-flows and discounts the balance of each year's net cash-flow to the present date by the relative costs thereby incurred.

BASF Pharma (the pharmaceutical division of BASF which was acquired by Abbott in March 2001) established the following methodology to evaluate projects (see Fig. 21). In order to traceably project revenues, a target-product profile has to be established first in collaboration with research, development and marketing departments. A target-profile is determined by the therapeutic area, impact-profile, scientific data for the registration authorities, competitive landscape, as well as the medical requirements and market expectations. Based upon the target-profile, a development plan can be derived including the necessary time-schedules, milestones, resources and activities, as well as – based on the marketing plan – the respective revenue expectations. This allows for the connection of qualitative factors (such as market attractiveness or competitive position) with quantitative factors (such as clinical data, market potential, market share, price expectations) in order to create cost-revenue plans and, hence, to set-up a free-cash-flow plan for each particular project. Simultaneously, a discussion and critical analysis of the departments that participate during the development (such as clinical development, marketing, production, authorization) is launched. The interdisciplinary appraisal of all available data and facts is the foremost reason for this step. The purpose of valuation is ultimately to gain an understanding and not to arrive at a number.

In order to generate the required data, only projects from the development stage 'clinical phase 2' onward will be included into the evaluation. At this point in time, the data available can describe and characterize the project in its respective market. This could include questions of the pharmacological impact-profile, which allow a firm to derive the therapeutic indication as well as assumptions about the daily dosages, which allow predicting detailed projections about prices and production.

The costs of production (without depreciation) are determined by using standard data, which are based upon average daily dosages according to clinical studies. The planning of the marketing costs is done simultaneously which can be derived from the respective marketing-mix. In case additional investments in property plant and equipment are necessary or a significant impact on the working capital can be expected (e.g., long payment horizons in the hospital business, in some European countries more than 1 or 2 years), they will have to be considered as 'cash out'. The calculated annual free-cash-flow is discounted by using the weighted-average cost of capital model. The planning horizon is about 10 to 15 years.

Novartis evaluates projects by comparing the potential value and expected performance of the projects. The potential value includes considerations about the market, competitiveness and/or feasibility. Performance parameters relate to the capabilities of the team, overall project objectives and the patent position among others. This approach is not only applicable to projects but also to technology platforms as well.

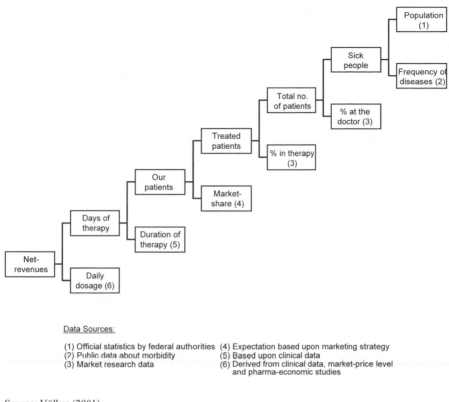

Data Sources:

(1) Official statistics by federal authorities   (4) Expectation based upon marketing strategy
(2) Public data about morbidity                  (5) Based upon clinical data
(3) Market research data                         (6) Derived from clinical data, market-price level
                                                     and pharma-economic studies

Source: Völker (2001)

**Fig. 21.** Determination of expected product revenues at BASF Pharma.

In some cases, R&D projects offer options that go beyond the actual project. For example, the development of a new product could be tied to the development of a new process, which has a certain probability to be used for the development of other products in the future. In situations like these, option-values have to be added to the direct value of a particular project. In recent years, the real options approach has frequently been discussed in valuing pharmaceutical R&D projects. However, due to its complexity it has not yet found broad acceptance or application in the industry.

Ultimately, portfolio management in pharmaceutical R&D requires a combination of risk-taking and risk-hedging. A full and solid pipeline of prospective products is the goal of every pharmaceutical company, and it is generally believed that the more new chemical entities pass through the pipeline and eventually enter the market, the better. However, the risk of market failure is increasing as most companies are targeting the same product areas and launching their products at closer intervals to each other. Markets are quickly crowded with competing products. For instance, the four angiotensin products Diovan, Teveten, Aprovel, and Atacand were introduced within a period of months. Therefore, a profound portfolio management system not only requires a focus on the number of new chemical entities, but also an adjustment in the way in which medicines are profiled and marketed. For example, Pfizer, for years did not use to pursue the strategy of being a leader in the number of market introductions but tried to maximize the commercial success of each new molecular entity. The company was very successful with this approach in the early 2000s. Hence, successful firms always allocate their resources, oftentimes via in-licensing agreements, to a limited number of high-value and innovative drugs which are expected to have significant sales potential. As pointed out before, the Holy Grail for any pharmaceutical company is to come up with a blockbuster product.

## The Disaggregation of the Pharmaceutical Value Chain

For many decades, pharmaceutical R&D has been a fully integrated process where the pharmaceutical company owned and conducted almost every single step of the R&D value chain. With the advent of open innovation, this full coverage seems neither desirable nor affordable. Instead of hiring the best people and doing everything oneself, firms increasingly concentrate on their core advantages and leverage outside innovators for their own innovation process (for open innovation, see Chesbrough 2003, 2006 and Gassmann 2006). The pharmaceutical industry used to be rather closed in its innovation models, partly due to the economies of scale which take place in new drug development.

However, since the 1990s, pharmaceutical companies also followed the trend toward more open innovation:

- Outsourcing of R&D;
- Joint ventures in R&D, typically focused on co-development or research for a special purpose or therapy area;
- Crowdsourcing: getting the best talents worldwide to solve a problem, e.g. Eli Lilly's research platform;
- Strategic alliances in research with complementary partners;
- In-licensing of intellectual property in later R&D stage, often from biotech firms;
- Out-licensing of research in the early R&D stages;

- Spin-offs and divestitures of R&D activities that are either not sufficiently promising or do not fit into the business strategy (e.g., because of a lack of marketing efforts).

In this context, most pharmaceutical companies have started to concentrate on their core competencies centering around technology platforms and therapy areas. They started to streamline their R&D activities deciding which tasks had to remain inside their own boundaries, and which tasks had to be absorbed from outside entities or could be multiplied by disposing them to external partners (Fig. 22). Balancing the right size and structure of the R&D department has turned out to be one of the primary issues in pharmaceutical R&D management.

In modern R&D, all functions are constantly analyzed regarding their potential contribution to shareholder value creation. This also raises the question about the definition of the corporate boundaries. Due to the increasing amount and number of interactions with outside innovation, every pharmaceutical company's R&D department today is more and more relying on some kind of external input from other companies or partner organizations.

The trend towards the externalization of (part of) a firm's R&D activities has led to the creation of several companies that provide innovators with technical and scientific services such as R&D contracts, laboratory testing services, technology consulting, industrial design, or even engineer-

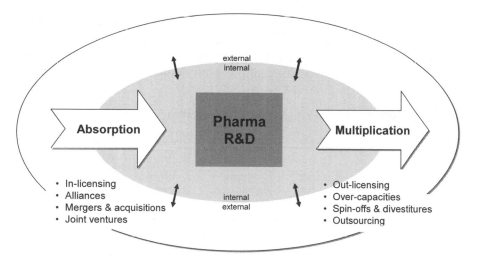

Source: Reepmeyer (2005)

**Fig. 22.** Restructuring of pharmaceutical R&D departments and resulting interaction with external partners.

ing. According to research by the OECD (2002), firms in high-technology R&D-intensive sectors, such as the pharmaceutical industry, have a high propensity to cooperate on innovation projects. The cascade of knowledge flowing from new sciences and technologies is simply far too complex for any company to handle alone. Fundamental breakthroughs are increasingly likely to occur not within a single firm's own R&D department but somewhere in an external organization's research lab.

As serendipity is still considered a key success factor particularly in the early discovery phases, a network with outside innovation is highly important in pharmaceutical R&D because the likelihood that a company generates all necessary substances in-house is relatively low. Interactions with partners not only reduce the risks implied in investing in the firm's own research infrastructure, but also the risks of a lack of access to the desired substances. Particularly the technology areas that are not yet covered by the pharmaceutical companies are subject to analysis of how they can best be accessed outside the corporate boundaries.

There are many different types of potential partnerships in the pharmaceutical industry. Due to the still highly integrated structure and value chain in the pharmaceutical industry, the closeness of the relationship between the pharmaceutical company and the external partner can serve as a criterion for the classification of the partners' interaction with the pharmaceutical company (Fig. 23). The nature of the interaction can embrace different attributes, features and forms depending on the commitment of resources. While in the case of outsourcing, the partner company usually conducts pre-defined tasks in return for a service fee, a collaboration refers to a more closely linked effort between both companies engaged in the joint project. This frequently involves risk, revenue and profit sharing agreements. In case of an integration, both companies' activities usually

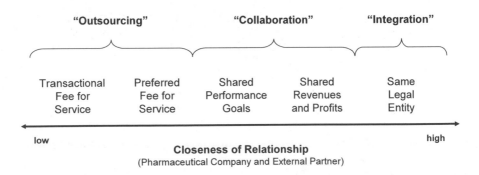

Source: Reepmeyer (2005)

**Fig. 23.** Classification of partnerships in pharmaceutical R&D activities.

melt together and there is no separation visible any more between both entities.

The reasons why firms establish alliances are usually multifold. According to Greis et al. (1995), the decision to engage in collaborations is usually based on the trade-off between inter-firm cooperation and vertical integration. This trade-off is seen as a comparison of transaction costs against development costs. When the organizational efficiency gains due to shared assets are greater than the production efficiency losses, a firm will choose to cooperate. The general explanation for the overall growth pattern of newly created R&D partnerships is mostly related to the motives that 'force' companies to collaborate on R&D. Major factors mentioned in that context are related to important industrial and technological changes that have led to increased complexity of scientific and technological development, higher uncertainty surrounding R&D, increasing costs of R&D projects, and shortened innovation cycles that favor collaboration.

The traditionally integrated structure of pharmaceutical R&D departments is expected to further decrease, and the interaction with external partners is increasing drastically. While the internal complexity of pharmaceutical R&D can thus be reduced, the complexity of managing relationships to external partners is escalating accordingly. The increasing reliance on outside innovation requires the pharmaceutical company to think and act in a more process-oriented way. Barriers between intra-organizational units as well as to external partners are expected to diminish. Only the pharmaceutical companies that are able to manage their R&D collaborations optimally will be capable to benefit from the novel developments and opportunities in the pharmaceutical industry.

## Impact of Outsourcing on Pharmaceutical R&D

Outsourcing represents the "loosest" form of cooperation between a pharmaceutical company and its partner firm. The rationale behind outsourcing usually refers to optimizing resources used in inhouse R&D. A market survey by Arthur D. Little and Solvias (2002) has shown that only lead finding, lead optimization and marketing are seen as core activities of pharmaceutical companies that have to be provided 100% in-house. All other activities are potential candidates for outsourcing, except for project management, which is a backbone process ensuring efficient know-how transfer between the different steps in pharmaceutical innovation. In fact, this outsourcing potential could have a major impact on the pharmaceutical value chain (Fig. 24).

INTEGRATED PHARMA COMPANY TODAY

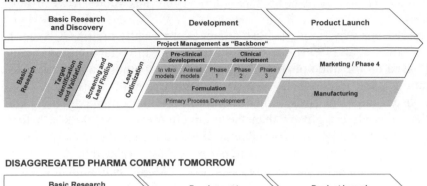

DISAGGREGATED PHARMA COMPANY TOMORROW

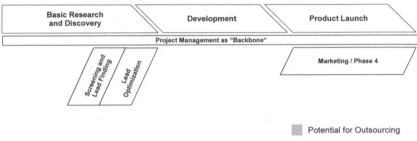

Potential for Outsourcing

**Fig. 24.** Impact of outsourcing on the pharmaceutical value chain according to Arthur D. Little.

Although outsourcing is controversially discussed in the pharmaceutical industry due to the high complexity in drug discovery, outsourcing some R&D activities to pharmaceutical service providers might lead to time and cost savings, would allow for access to new technologies and know-how and could help manage peak resource shortages. Many pharmaceutical companies already work with multiple outsourcing partners during the in-novation process to build greater experience in managing value networks rather than just value chains. Besides biotechnology, genomics-based and other platform companies, these partners include a wide variety of contract service organizations (CSOs). The term CSO includes contract research organizations (CRO), contract manufacturing organizations (CMO), site management organizations (SMO), and any other organization that pro-vides pharmaceutical companies with a contract service. Research by Lehman Brothers (1999) has shown that contract research organizations are able to conduct clinical trials up to 30 percent faster than the average large pharmaceutical company. In 1999, pharmaceutical companies spent about 25 percent of their R&D budgets for services provided by CROs.

This number is expected to increase to about 40 percent (see Lehman Brothers 1999). At this stage, the CRO industry consists of over 1,000 companies based in the US, Europe and Asia. There are many rather small CROs which usually are regionally embedded into local market structures.

The entire market for pharmaceutical R&D outsourcing was US$ 9.3 billion in 2001 and is predicted to reach US$ 36 billion by 2010. This represents an annual growth rate of 16.3 percent compared to an average expected growth in global R&D expenditure of 9.6 percent during the same period (Reuters 2003c). Most of this outsourced effort is being expended on non-clinical drug development, clinical trials, and manufacturing aspects of the drug development process.

Outsourcing requires the pharmaceutical company to think and act in a more process-oriented way. Barriers between intra-organizational units as well as to external partners are expected to diminish. External experts could either be integrated into the innovation process for a limited time or they could just provide some necessary infrastructure and basic services to the pharmaceutical company. Primary drivers for outsourcing include:

- Reduction of over-capacities (as a result of M&A activity);
- Cost cutting or restructuring issues;
- Growth aspirations (expertise, resources);
- Reduction of risk and/or proactive risk management;
- Corporate governance and/or strategic make-or-by decision.

The final decision to outsource R&D functions usually depends on many different parameters (see also Festel and Polastro 2002):

- Technological requirements and specifications (technologies and synthesis techniques, available capacities, status of registration);
- Product-specific considerations (quantity, position within the lifecycle, impact on the overall product portfolio);
- Financial aspects (investments, economic feasibility: in-house production vs. outsourced production);
- Taxes (the access to medical substances is oftentimes used in order to optimize the tax load);
- Market access (despite new developments, the pharmaceutical industry is still characterized by a more or less open protectionism);
- 'Chemical' tradition of the pharmaceutical company (philosophy, commitment to chemical processes).

If a pharmaceutical company intends to outsource some part of its R&D activities to an external service provider, three questions are important (see Arthur D. Little, Solvias 2002):

- What kind of services could potentially be interesting for R&D outsourcing?
- What are the most effective and efficient interfaces between the pharmaceutical company and the service provider?
- Which cooperation models are the best basis for managing the outsourcing activities?

The kind of activities that could be outsourced to service providers is usually dependant upon the characteristics of the pharmaceutical company. It has been shown that big pharmaceutical companies, mid-size pharmaceutical companies and start-ups usually adopt different outsourcing strategies.

Big pharmaceutical companies are typically involved in outsourcing activities for strategic reasons. In the early phases, this includes such things as process development, scale-up and delivery of first lot sizes for clinical trials. The goal is to circumvent bottlenecks in one's own development process and to manage peak resource shortages. Mid-size pharmaceutical companies usually concentrate on one or two products emanating from their own R&D pipeline. While outsourcing structures of mid-size pharmaceutical companies are typically comparable to big pharmaceutical companies, the major difference is the low proportion of outsourced substances of older compounds. Hence, the focus of contract-synthesis lies more on advanced intermediate products rather than on substances. Start-ups, as the third type of pharmaceutical companies, are typically very much characterized by limited capacities in synthesis development and production. As a result, they could almost entirely have to rely on outsourcing and, hence, represent a huge market for pharmaceutical service providers.

While outsourcing in pharmaceutical R&D is extremely complex, managing the outsourcing partner can be very cumbersome depending on the field of collaboration. Thus, many companies still use outsourcing only to manage peak resource shortages despite its potential to help improve overall R&D performance.

Novel objects for outsourcing may include that the pharmaceutical company itself could actively support outsourcing activities by making financial investments into legal entities that serve as an outsourcing partner. A good example for the latter case is the Novartis Venture Fund which provides capital for spin-offs in order to reduce non-needed capacities and release entrepreneurial responsibility and capability. Among others, the Novartis Venture Fund funded the Novartis spin-off Solvias which is now a highly important outsourcing partner for Novartis.

**Novartis Venture Fund**

The Novartis Venture Fund was founded in 1996 and supports new business projects that show entrepreneurial spirit in the health science areas. Today, the Novartis Venture Fund is one of the largest corporate biotech venture funds with more than US$ 500 million under management. Since the Funds' inception, 98 companies were funded (shareholdings), and 60 companies have been part of the equity portfolio at the end of 2006. The entire fund is comprised of three different funds: the Spin-off Fund, the Start-up Fund, and the BioVenture Fund.

The mission of the Spin-off Fund is to support, coach and facilitate Novartis spin-offs on a worldwide basis. In most cases the Fund provides seed money to support employees who want to create their own business, based on a convincing business plan. The Start-up Fund supports entrepreneurship and investments in start-up companies mainly from European universities. The Fund offers seed money, but frequently assists the companies throughout further financing rounds. The objective of the BioVenture Fund is to invest in product- and platform-focused biotechnology, pharmaceutical and healthcare companies at all stages, with an emphasis on the United States. The Novartis Venture Fund supports companies worldwide, for example in Switzerland, the US, and Singapore. In Novartis' hometown Basel and the surrounding area alone, the Novartis Venture Fund has helped establish 25 companies which so far generate combined annual revenues of about CHF 125 million and created roughly 800 jobs.

## Rising Importance of R&D Collaborations

Besides of outsourcing, pharmaceutical companies frequently enter into collaborations with external partners. As illustrated in Fig. 25, more than 600 alliances worldwide are formed annually between pharmaceutical and biotechnology firms with a total value of over US$ 30 billion in 2004 (see Recombinant Capital 2005). Several large pharmaceutical companies spend significant amounts of their R&D budgets on collaboration agreements. Aventis spends a total of 15 percent of its R&D budget on collaborations. One third (i.e. 5% of the total R&D budget) goes into technology partnerships in early research, discovery and screening, and two thirds (i.e. 10% of the total R&D budget) goes into development collaborations across

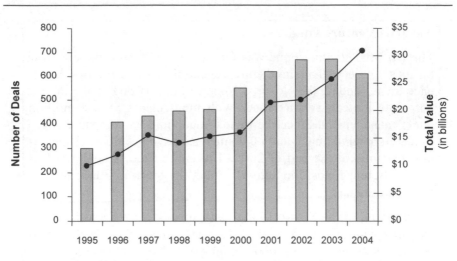

Source: Recombinant Capital (2005)

**Fig. 25.** Development of alliances in the pharmaceutical industry.

all clinical stages, particularly Phase II. Novartis has reserved about 20 to 25 percent of its research budget for extramural research and this percentage is on the rise (Herrling 1998).

Of 691 new chemical entities approved by the FDA from 1963 to 1999, 38 percent evolved out of alliances. In accordance, the average number of biotech alliances per pharmaceutical firm grew from 1.4 per year in the period 1988 through 1990 to 5.7 in 1997 through 1998. In addition, the probability of a drug passing through human testing which has been developed jointly increases by up to 30 percentage points over drugs developed by a single firm alone (see Nicholson, Danzon and McCullough 2003).

The increasingly rapid pace of innovation in the pharmaceutical industry calls for more flexible and looser forms of innovation agreements. In accordance, today's pharmaceutical R&D collaborations not only cover the typically technology-intensive research collaborations, but increasingly include various contractual partnership agreements, such as co-development or co-promotion agreements. Particularly the majority of the novel niche-markets can oftentimes only be entered successfully in partnership with specialized companies. Therefore, many pharmaceutical companies have started to engage in collaboration agreements with various partners to gain access to the different niche-markets and to utilize an external partner's special sales force capabilities as illustrated by the case of Prometheus.

**Prometheus: How a small company's sales force can be attractive to big pharma companies**

Prometheus is a small specialty pharmaceutical company based in San Diego, CA. Prometheus has built a unique commercialization platform from which it launches its specialty pharmaceuticals based on providing a continuum of care in gastroenterology. Prometheus offers other technologically sophisticated diagnostic services, all geared to help gastroenterologists deliver optimal therapies for inflammatory disease (which includes Crohn's disease and ulcerative colitis). According to Windhover (2000), Prometheus' then Chairman Michael Walsh says "ultimately, this technology is part of a strategy for differentiating the sales and commercialization process. We have a field sales force of 50, calling on the 4,500 high-prescribing, high patient volume physicians. Our people end up with 20-30 minutes in the clinician's office, instead of the 2 minutes that reps in other specialties spend near the sample cabinet." Prometheus' sales representatives lead a consultative sale that doctors welcome, because they help physicians provide a continuum of care from early detection and diagnosis to drug therapy. This commercialization strategy is rarely applied by big pharmaceutical companies which solely rely on mass-marketing of high volume drugs. As a result, Prometheus positioned itself as an attractive sales partner in this specialty niche.

Many companies decide to choose alliances not only to access new markets but also to accelerate the market diffusion of their new products. Particularly for selling new medicines on a global scale, it seems to be a promising approach to team up with a partner who already has broad expertise, deep knowledge or special access to the targeted market, and who is most likely capable to improve the product launch in the desired market. For example, many U.S. and European companies typically introduce their new drugs on the Japanese market only in collaboration with a local pharmaceutical company. The pharmaceutical companies usually expect that the aspired higher sales generated by the collaboration will overcompensate for the loss in revenues that go to the alliance partner.

The nature of a successful collaboration requires that both partners' success is based on the success of the joint project. The fortunes of both parties in the R&D collaboration must be inextricably linked: both companies gain or lose together, and each partner has to look at the other partner's success as their own success. Both sides of the R&D collaboration should be highly incentivized to turn the mutually developed substance into a success. Linking the performance of both partners in the collaboration to the joint project's performance seems to represent a new paradigm in pharmaceutical R&D collaborations. It could have been observed that this type of performance-conjunction is manifested in the nature of many of today's pharmaceutical R&D collaborations. Performance-based structures are unambiguously on the rise. The amount of milestone payments in pharmaceutical R&D (i.e. payments based on the mutual achievement of certain goals) outperformed upfront payments by far over the last 10 years, reaching more than US$ 90 billion in 2004 compared to around US$ 12 billion in upfront payments for the same year (Recombinant Capital 2005).

As successful collaborations by their nature always center around sharing certain property rights or markets, they require both partners to contribute a certain part of the joint work. Therefore, the different types of collaborations in pharmaceutical R&D can be classified according to two criteria: the work that is contributed to the collaboration by the pharmaceutical company, and the work that is contributed by the external partner. Based on the perspective of the pharmaceutical company, this classification results in four different types of R&D collaboration (see Fig. 26):

- Research alliance;
- In-licensing;
- Co-development;
- Out-licensing.

Whereas research alliances, in-licensing, and co-development are quite established and traditional collaboration approaches, out-licensing has long been considered a difficult task by many established pharmaceutical companies. The different types of R&D collaboration are discussed in detail in the following chapters.

## Research Alliances: Accessing Early-stage Innovation

In case of research alliances, both partners focus on issues related to basic research and drug discovery. They usually intend to come up with new targets or compounds by leveraging their individual technology platforms, know-how or capital.

Typical research alliances of pharmaceutical companies include target identification partnerships with biotech firms. Due to the fact that most biotech firms have no product on the market yet and, hence, are heavily reliant on their research activities, they are of particular interest to estab-

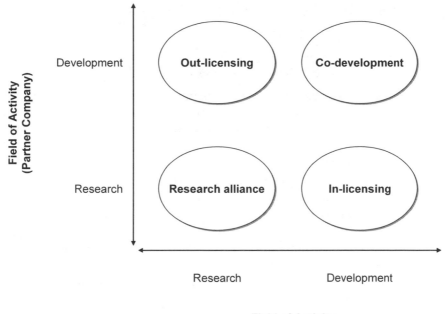

Source: Reepmeyer (2005)

**Fig. 26.** Different types of collaboration in pharmaceutical R&D (perspective: pharmaceutical company).

lished pharmaceutical companies' R&D. While biotech firms usually react very quickly to novel technology changes and deploy the latest scientific and technological equipment, pharmaceutical companies are better off in partnering rather than competing with them. Indeed, recent research has shown that new biotech firms have not replaced incumbent pharmaceutical firms, but both prefer a symbiotic coexistence (Rothaermel 2001).

The biotech firms' rationale to enter research alliances with large pharmaceutical companies is to access distribution channels as well as capital for the cost-intensive clinical development activities. They also seek partnerships with established pharmaceutical firms because a collaboration with a large pharmaceutical player increases the biotech firm's credibility. The technological know-how is mostly too complex to communicate to all stakeholders. A collaboration with a brand-name pharmaceutical company is a strong credential for the quality of the biotech's research (Robbins-Roth 2001). On the other hand, research alliances also provide the established pharmaceutical companies with several advantages. The two most important advantages are as follows (see Herrling 1998):

- It can acquire first-hand knowledge and expertise in a new technology;
- It has time to see whether the technology has a real therapeutic future.

If the collaboration seems to be promising, the pharmaceutical company can eventually acquire the external partner to get exclusive access to the technologies and know-how. Hence, research alliances extend the pharmaceutical companies' reach at relatively low costs and risks compared to the acquisition approach.

Today, large pharmaceutical companies typically work in huge research networks covering up to several hundreds of biotechnology firms. The relation of the collaborations is mostly bilateral with the pharmaceutical company being the hub of the network. Sometimes, a third partner enters the bilateral collaborations between the pharmaceutical and the biotech company in order to provide the necessary application environment. A network among the biotech firms mostly does not exist (see also Becker et al. 1999). Acquisitions or a majority ownership by the pharmaceutical companies are rare, even if the Swiss companies Novartis (now owns 100% of Chiron) and Roche (owns a 60% stake in Genentech) are examples for the latter case. One of the most prominent examples of a research alliance has been the Bayer-Millennium collaboration that was initiated in the late 1990s.

---

**Research alliance at Bayer**

Between 1998 and 2003, Bayer invested a total amount of around US$ 465 million into a research partnership with Millennium. This investment included an equity investment of US$ 96.6 million for a 14 percent stake in Millennium. Bayer's intention was to use Millennium's genomics-related technology platform to discover 225 new genomics-based drug targets. At the end of this purely research-oriented collaboration, more than 450 drug targets could have been identified for Bayer by Millennium. In addition, Bayer was able to sell its interest in Millennium for approximately US$ 300 million which is equivalent to a multiple of 3x of the initial investment. While both parties regarded the collaboration as a success, the industry remains skeptical about the alliance's results: only one validated pre-clinical drug candidate emerged out of all drug targets that had been identified during this research alliance.

---

## In-licensing: Enhancing the Innovation Pipeline

In-licensing has emerged as a key value driver for pharmaceutical companies. Industry leaders have recognized in-licensing as a strategic mechanism through which they can achieve their corporate objectives. In the case of in-licensing, the pharmaceutical company (licensee) acquires intellectual property of a third party (licensor), and expects that this intellectual property fills a gap in its own development pipeline. Examples of tradable intellectual property rights include specific biotechnological procedures (i.e. platform technologies) or compounds. Typical applications of intellectual property are databases or software in which the licensor provides the respective know-how. Distinctive 'knowledge-service packages' can thus be created and actively marketed. Indeed, patents on novel biotechnological achievements are usually not used to secure the knowledge, but to purposely sell the knowledge. Even research results which are not directly related to a specific R&D activity obtain a certain value and can be marketed. In some cases, complex co-marketing agreements are signed along with the in-licensing deal.

The most important reasons why it may be desirable or necessary for a pharmaceutical company to in-license intellectual property from external third parties include:

- Quick expansion of the portfolio of potential drug candidates without the risks and costs involved in a substantial research and development program;
- Better and more flexible utilization of development capacities which makes the financial risk more calculable.
- High complement of the in-licensed technologies with those developed in-house (e.g., a business with a promising anti-cancer drug might seek a license of a third party's drug delivery technology to enhance its own product);
- Access to rights in platform technologies and software products to assist in research and drug development. Pharmaceutical companies often prefer to focus their resources on the later stages of development and commercialization once the potential of a product or technology has been identified, where the financial rewards are clearer;
- Avoidance of infringement action by a third party. As it is not always possible to work around a patent, negotiating a license and in-licensing it can be the only way to avoid an expensive and potentially disastrous infringement claim.

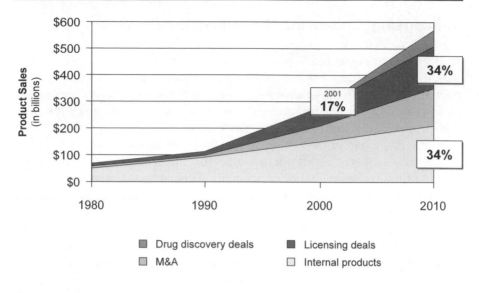

Source: Wood Mackenzie (2003b)

**Fig. 27.** Rising proportion of sales from in-licensed products.

The pharmaceutical companies' desire to in-license objects developed elsewhere has experienced tremendous growth. Payments for in-licensing have quadrupled for products in early and late stages of development. Average payments have increased, with the largest increase for drugs entering the mid-stage trials.

In addition, nine of the top ten pharmaceutical companies have in-licensed more than 40 percent of their marketed new molecular entities. Most of the compounds were in clinical stages I and II (Cap Gemini Ernst & Young 2001). In 2000, 14 of the top 55 drugs by sales were in-licensed (Accenture 2002). For example, a few years ago, all of Bristol-Myers Squibb's blockbuster products (Pravachol, Taxol, Glucophage, Plavix and Avapro) were the result of in-licensing (MedAd News 2000). GlaxoSmithKline in-licensed nine compounds in 2001 alone all of them targeting major therapy areas.

Overall, in-licensed products accounted for 17 percent of pharmaceutical sales in 2001, and this number is expected to grow to 34 percent by 2010 (see Fig. 27). According to research by Wood Mackenzie (2003b), sales contributed by in-licensed products will then equal sales achieved by internally developed products.

---

**In-licensing at Pfizer**

Probably the most prominent example of an in-licensed drug is Pfizer's Lipitor. Pfizer marketed Lipitor (initially on behalf of Warner-Lambert before the company had been acquired by Pfizer) to compete with drugs such as Zocor (Merck), Pravachol (Bristol-Myers Squibb), and Lipobay (Bayer) for the lucrative cholesterol-lowering drug market. Lipitor was originally in-licensed from Yamanouchi. Pfizer then used its marketing strength and sales capabilities to turn this externally sourced 'me-too' drug into the most successful blockbuster ever. In 2003, Lipitor became the first pharmaceutical product ever that topped US$ 10 billion in annual sales. Today, Lipitor generates well above US$ 13 billion in revenues, although it faces patent expiration in 2009.

---

The increasing prominence of in-licensing has led to ever more complex contractual arrangements. Unidirectional one-time payments have been replaced by sophisticated and timely limited agreements, which typically cover different geographical markets. Success premiums, milestone payments, and royalty agreements oftentimes increase the contractual complexity. The extent of the performance-oriented contractual arrangement usually depends on the risk-benefit profile of the collaboration. The earlier the stage of the collaboration, the more difficult it is to calculate prospective revenue streams. Many licensors thus reserve the right to market the developed drug in certain strategically important markets by themselves.

In summary, in-licensing of lead substances which have not been discovered internally provides pharmaceutical firms with a vehicle to obtain promising drug candidates while it leaves the risk of the initial discovery to an external partner. Therefore, this type of R&D collaboration not only helps the pharmaceutical firm reduce the risks implied in investments in the company's own research and discovery infrastructure, but also the risks of a lack of access to the desired substances to fill its own development pipeline. In-licensing always includes the transfer of property rights and, therefore, links the success of the partners to the success of the joint effort.

## Co-development: Mutually Benefiting from Joint Resources

Co-development agreements refer to the mutual development of a drug. This approach is mostly used by companies that try to complement their development and marketing capabilities. For example, a biotechnology company which already has a substance in clinical development but does not own a sales force in an important market, teams up with a larger company to jointly develop the last stages of the drug and to sell it mutually after registration. The development is usually conducted by joint teams. One of the earliest examples of a co-development agreement between a pharmaceutical company and a biotechnology firm is the collaboration of Eli Lilly and Genentech which entered into a joint initiative to develop the recombinant human insulin already in 1977.

For many companies, the need to collaborate in development is typically driven by a particular project need or by specific market circumstances. The increasing disintegration of the R&D process and the growing need to develop innovative drugs across various platforms and therapy areas both drive companies towards this collaborative approach. However, a few companies are now pushing beyond that point, making co-development an integral element of their business model and realizing significant gains in the effectiveness and efficiency of R&D.

---

**Co-development at Aventis**

In 2001, Aventis Pharmaceuticals (the U.S. subsidiary of Aventis S.A.) entered into a collaboration agreement with Altana Pharma (then known as Byk Gulden) regarding the joint development of the substance Alvesco®. The substance was initially developed by Byk Gulden. Subsequently to the agreement, Aventis was developing the drug candidate exclusively for the U.S. market. In 2004, Aventis received market approval for Alvesco® in the U.S. and started to market the product. Aventis will compensate Altana Pharma in return for providing the substance by conveying a certain percentage of the drug's revenues incurred in the US. In Europe, Altana Pharma continued to develop the drug and will market it. Altana Pharma reached EU market approval for Alvesco® in 2005.

Aventis' intention to enter the co-development with Altana Pharma was to close a gap in its product pipeline and to improve the company's product portfolio. Altana Pharma's intention to enter the co-development with Aventis was to make use of Aventis' presence in the U.S. to ensure a proper market introduction of the drug in the U.S. market. As the story of Alvesco® is considered a success by both partners, Aventis and Altana Pharma were both able to reduce their exposure to risks – related to growth aspirations and market introduction respectively – by jointly developing the substance.

---

The integration of the processes by which work gets done and decisions are made are the key elements to co-development activities. For example, Aventis also engaged into a 50/50 co-development partnership with Millennium. A main aspect of this collaboration is the mutual commitment that if one company's task gets completed faster than expected, the partners may shift more tasks to that company to both equalize resource time and accelerate progress of the program (see Deck and Strom 2002). The monetary incentives for the partners to join co-development are usually upfront payments, milestone payments, as well as royalty payments after the drug successfully reached the market. Particularly revenue sharing is an important aspect of co-development agreements. Co-development is generally done to accelerate development times. The new drug is therefore able to enter the market sooner than in the case of stand-alone development which is expected to lead to higher returns even after the partner firm has received the stipulated proportion of the revenues incurred.

Co-development agreements can cover many different areas. A recent co-development agreement between Aventis and Pfizer, for example, implies that Pfizer develops a certain insulin drug and Aventis helps provide the investments necessary to build up the production capacity. In general, success factors for co-development cover the following aspects:

- Development of a business-based co-development strategy based on each partners' strengths;
- Identification of the skill gaps relative to the resources needed for the co-development relationship;
- Definition of a process and set of criteria for evaluating and selecting development partners;
- Assignment of an active sponsor for each co-development relationship;
- Alignment of expectations of the partners and clarification how the relationship will actually work in a joint development agreement;
- Determination that each co-development deliverable has a clear, common definition across organizations;
- Establishment of explicit, direct communication linkages between development teams within and across organizations;
- Access to information tools for the development teams to enable secure, real-time information flow between companies including the establishment of processes and organizational elements that facilitate the use of those tools;
- Introduction of regular intervals to measure and assess the progress of each co-development relationship.

In summary, pharmaceutical firms prefer co-development collaborations in order to utilize the development and marketing capabilities of another firm. As biotech companies increasingly contribute late-stage compounds to their collaborations with established pharmaceutical companies, their improved negotiation power enables them to get involved in co-development agreements as well. The large pharmaceutical company can thus share development risks as the partner company has already or is about to contribute development activities to the joint project. Both firms usually share the benefits of a successful market entry via royalty revenue or profit sharing agreements.

## Out-licensing: Commercializing Internal Research Results

> *"I say it all of the time – and I mean it – a medicine that sits on the shelf helps no one."*
>
> *Billy Tauzin,*
> *President and CEO, PhRMA*

While research alliances, in-licensing and co-development have been common collaboration approaches of most established pharmaceutical companies for several years, out-licensing has long been considered a difficult task for large pharmaceutical companies. While out-licensing as a phenomenon is as new as in-licensing (it is the same as in-licensing but from a reversed perspective), its utilization by large and established pharmaceutical companies, however, is fairly novel. Some large pharmaceutical companies – including Eli Lilly, Schering, Bayer, Roche or Novartis – have only recently adopted this R&D collaboration strategy.

### Reasons for the pharmaceutical companies' resistance towards out-licensing

One of the most frequently mentioned reasons why pharmaceutical companies have been reluctant for so many years to apply the concept of out-licensing includes that 'no one will win any awards within a large drug company for a successful out-licensing deal that generates some upfront and modest expectations for royalties in the distant future' (see Windhover 2003). An even bigger obstacle to out-licensing by pharmaceutical companies is the realization that selling off rights to an unrecognized blockbuster could be a career-ending move for the respective executive. According to Windhover (2000), most large pharmaceutical companies are fairly uncomfortable about relinquishing control of their drugs because they fear that selling products will leave gaping holes in their revenues. In addition, R&D management also has to deal with employees' emotions affixed to killing a project which they worked on for several years. However, according to information by Merck KGaA, it is oftentimes the case that employees are even happy if another company is willing to continue a project which the out-licensing company did/could not want to pursue any further.

Another reason why many pharmaceutical companies have been reluctant to out-license their compounds has usually been that no one would consider a compound to have any value if a big pharmaceutical company – which has the necessary infrastructure to bring a compound to the market – decided to terminate the respective R&D project. Research by Kollmer and Dowling (2004) supports this perspective. The authors figured out in a study on licensing in the biopharmaceutical industry that fully integrated firms out-license only their non-core products. The reasons are usually a misfit with their overall strategy although – considering their size – they could bring these products to the market independently. Many companies seem to fail to recognize that most R&D projects are terminated due to reasons which are not related to the compound itself. In this context, Bayer particularly highlights – when the company intends to out-license a substance – that 'this is most likely a Bayer-specific problem rather than a problem of the substance'. However, instead of acknowledging the fact that the terminated drug candidate still has a certain therapeutic value, many industry participants used to believe that the underlying compound had a negative connotation. The study by Kollmer and Dowling (2004) contradicts this belief and even highlights the potential of out-licensing at large pharmaceutical companies. The results of their research show that the out-licensing activities of fully integrated firms bring comparable compensation to that of not-fully integrated firms, even though the former mostly out-license non-core products. In both cases, licensing seems to be a profitable business.

Research by Recombinant Capital (2005) involving 2,623 alliances forged by the top 20 pharmaceutical companies with biotechnology companies between 1988 and 2002 supports the still existing resistance of large pharmaceutical companies to out-license their compounds: only 1 out of 8 alliances is an out-licensing deal by a pharmaceutical company. However, despite its fairly low contribution in absolute terms, out-licensing by pharmaceutical companies has experienced remarkable growth over the past few years (Fig. 28). While the total number of out-licensing deals between 2000 and 2002 is still small (81) compared to, for example, thera-

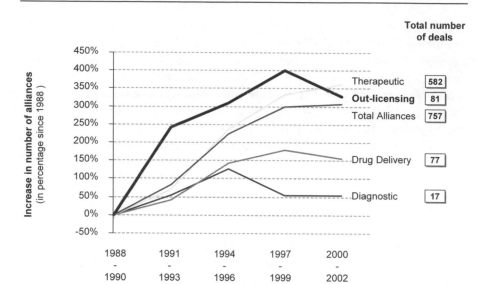

Source: Recombinant Capital (2005)

**Fig. 28.** Growth in alliances of top 20 pharma companies (1988 to 2002).

peutic alliances during the same time period (582), the growth of out-licensing deals outperformed the increase of most other types of alliances including the average of all alliances, although it has recently experienced a small slow-down. This tremendous growth is a strong indicator for the huge potential behind out-licensing.

## Potential of out-licensing

As out-licensing strategies utilize external resources for the further development of internally developed substances, out-licensing always promotes the dissemination of technologies and products by integrating a company's intellectual property with complementary assets. Therefore, out-licensing should be adopted by companies which possess a strong position in a certain technology area but lack the complementary assets necessary to exploit the technology (see Fig. 29). Successfully executed out-licensing programs provide the pharmaceutical firm with several benefits, such as additional revenue generation, cost and resource effectiveness, or mitigation of R&D related risks. Megantz (2002) states that out-licensing lowers risks because less investment and fewer resources are needed; much of the risk remains largely offloaded onto the partner company, who is responsi-

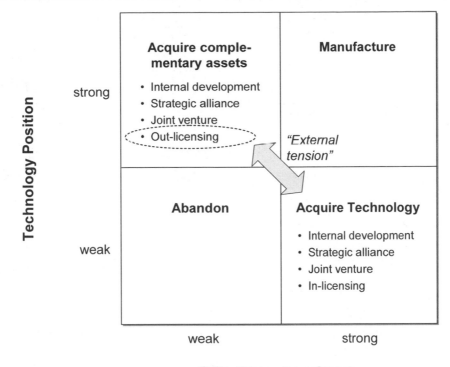

Source: compare Megantz (2002)

**Fig. 29.** Out-licensing: The neglected strategy to gain complementary assets for the utilization of a company's own technology.

ble for the further development of the licensed product. If a product fails or a strategy changes, the pharmaceutical company can usually simply walk away without any undesirable follow-up operation. Only some usually small termination fees might occur.

A study by IBM (2003) about licensing in the pharmaceutical industry revealed that the objects that are licensed in out-licensing deals usually cover new molecular entities (see Fig. 30). The study concludes that most out-licensors are responding with their licensing offers to the needs of the current marketplace.

The most important reasons why it may be advantageous or necessary for a pharmaceutical company to out-license intellectual property to a third party include the following aspects:

• No intended internal usage any more for the technology, compound, or intellectual property;

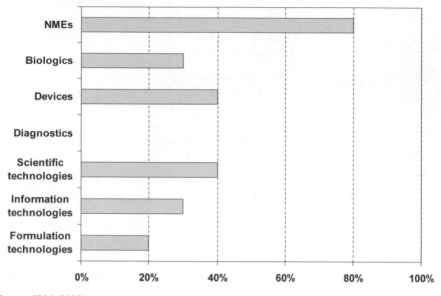

Source: IBM (2003)

**Fig. 30.** Product responsibility of the business development & licensing departments at pharmaceutical companies regarding out-licensing.

- Lack of resources and/or internal expertise for further exploitation;
- The risk profile of the substance and/or compound does not match the internal requirements;
- Specialization on certain product areas or technologies, such as a portfolio restructuring;
- Exploitation of therapy areas other than initially intended therapy areas (e.g., a pharmaceutical company only plans to develop a product or technology in one therapy area, but this product may have applications in other areas; this could even include areas which go beyond pharmaceuticals, such as cosmetics or plant breeding);
- Lack of commercialization potential (e.g., the drug's target market is considered to be insufficient in size to justify further R&D investments);
- Low-risk opportunity to move into new, complementary or unknown markets;
- Improvement of the company's revenue stream and/or market penetration by focusing on short-term income;
- Expansion of geographical reach;
- Side benefits, such as increased brand visibility because of advertising by the licensee or the use of improvements developed by the licensee;

- Maximization of the firm's asset utilization and value of the drug port-folio by leveraging internal R&D capacities;
- Gaining advantages in non-core markets by selling non-core technologies;
- Testing a market that may later be exploited by direct investments.

Probably the most important benefit of out-licensing includes that the pharmaceutical company could increase the utilization rate of its internal research results without using significant additional resources. As soon as the pharmaceutical company has made the decision not to continue the further development of a compound internally any more, the pharmaceutical company could find new avenues to commercialize its intellectual assets at the respective stages of the R&D process. This requires the abandonment of the traditional path of commercialization, and the creation of a new market for the compound (see Fig. 31). An external partner's R&D re-

**TRADITIONAL COMMERCIALIZATION PROCESS IN THE PHARMACEUTICAL INDUSTRY**

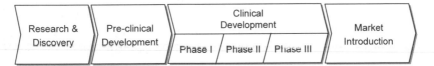

**NOVEL COMMERCIALIZATION PROCESS BASED ON OUT-LICENSING**

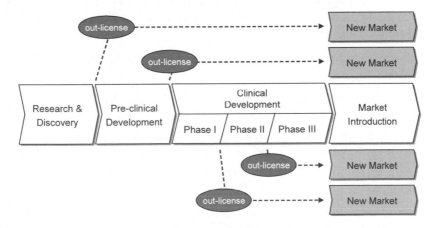

Source: Reepmeyer (2005)

**Fig. 31.** Out-licensing as a way to open new markets.

sources could be utilized to bring the compound to the market instead of letting the compound decay inside the pharmaceutical company's R&D boundaries.

Selling the rights for further development of a compound to an external partner not only helps transfer R&D risks but also allows the generation of royalty revenues in case the licensed compound reaches the market at some point in the future. The following case example illustrates how Bayer handles out-licensing deals.

---

**Out-licensing at Bayer**

Bayer's primary intention to pursue out-licensing of compounds is to gain additional revenues for something which has already caused irreversible R&D costs and would otherwise be terminated without any further commercialization.

Bayer considers the grant of the IND (Investigational New Drug) approval to be an important milestone before a substance can be effectively licensed out. The IND approval is filed with the FDA prior to the clinical trials of a new drug (i.e. before the substance enters the human body and after it has completed the pre-clinical studies). It already gives a full and comprehensive description of the new drug. The IND is followed by the NDA (New Drug Application) . As development is responsible for filing INDs at Bayer, most out-licensing agreements at Bayer are done by the development department which means that most substances are licensed out at a relatively late stage of the R&D process. However, Bayer also recently started to license out and utilize early-stage substances of its research department.

The reasons for Bayer to out-license a substance include several aspects:

*The number of patients that the drug candidate is expected to reach.* If the number of patients seems to turn out lower than estimated, the drug's potential is consequently less attractive. Bayer then considers out-licensing the compound hoping to find a licensing partner who finds the drug candidate attractive despite the smaller size of the target market.

*The drug's compliance.* If a competitor is about to launch a similar product which has a better compliance, Bayer considers omitting the drug and licensing out the compound.

*The drug's administration.* A lack of convenience for the patient might be a reason for Bayer to stop pursuing a new drug. In case a competitor introduces a similar drug which can be administered to the patient in a more convenient way (e.g., orally via tablets vs. injections), Bayer usually intends to stop the drug's development and chooses the option of out-licensing. An external partner might find a different application for the substance which could turn it into a success on a different market.

*The price projection.* If the prospective price of the future drug may drop and won't meet the initial assumptions any more, and it becomes apparent that the estimated sales projections may not be achieved, Bayer intends to out-license the substance as well. Another company could have different sales channels or target markets which might make the drug attractive to them.

*Reimbursement by the health insurance companies.* If a new drug is about to be reimbursed by health insurances, far more drugs can usually be sold than without any support by health insurances. By contrast, if the health insurances do not reimburse the patients, the new drug might not seem as attractive to Bayer any more because the projected number of sold units probably cannot be achieved. In this case, Bayer usually stops pursuing the drug candidate, but a licensing partner might still find the compound useful for its own pipeline.

A critical aspect of any out-licensing agreement is the licensor's ability to retain an interest in the licensed compound's future performance. As the estimation of a drug's potential is very complex and characterized by a high uncertainty, mistakes in evaluating the potential of a substance could have a high price in terms of opportunity costs if the pharmaceutical firm is unable to benefit from the drug's upside potential any more. As most pharmaceutical companies are afraid to miss out on the opportunity of participating in a drug's upside potential, they typically do not get involved in an out-licensing deal if they won't be allowed to retain certain re-licensing rights. The most frequently used re-licensing right in practice is the call-back option.

For example, Aventis failed to recognize the potential of one of its products when the firm sold it for a relatively low price to King Pharmaceuticals without retaining any stakes in the drug's future potential.

**Aventis: Call-back options would prevent missing out on a compound's upside**

The specialty pharmaceutical company King Pharmaceuticals acquired the drug Ramipril (altace), an angiotensin-converting enzyme (ACE) inhibitor, in 1998 from Aventis as part of a package of three drugs costing US$ 363 million (see Thiel 2004). Aventis sold the drug because it was not clearly differentiated from other products in this crowded therapeutic field.

After a subsequent study conducted by King Pharmaceuticals, which proved that the drug reduced risk of death from stroke and heart attack in certain populations, the drug got additional labeling that certified its uniqueness. King Pharmaceuticals generated US$ 527 million in sales with the drug Altace in 2003 alone. Because Aventis did not have any stakes in the drug any more, the company missed out on this great opportunity just because its judgment about the drug's potential was wrong. King's management only faced marketing risks – the prospect that they would never be able to get the expected sales out of what looked like a me-too ACE inhibitor – but they did not have to worry about getting the product into the pharmacies because it had already been in the U.S. market for seven years.

Most established pharmaceutical companies today still use out-licensing only as a tactical tool. They only out-license compounds that did not make it into the company's top priority list. However, not only terminated compounds but potentially any compound that can be developed more efficiently by an external partner could become subject to an out-licensing agreement. A more strategic approach to out-licensing could help improve not only the image of compounds that are out-licensed by large pharmaceutical companies but also the effectiveness of internal R&D.

A more progressive approach to the commercialization of research results could be implemented if the respective out-licensing activities receive clear profit and loss responsibilities. Out-licensing could be organized as a profit center with a clear mission: To increase the utilization of corporate research. For example, Schering started in fiscal year 2004 – for the first time ever – to incorporate out-licensing as an independent item in the company's budget calculations. Being a pioneer in out-licensing, Eli Lilly is reported to have achieved around US$ 2 billion from its out-licensing activities over the last five years.

# How to Commercialize a Breakthrough Technology

As an illustration of a partnership between two companies to exploit the full potential of a new technology, the following case describes the commercialization of InnoGel™, a breakthrough soft capsule technology, and covers in detail the structure of the commercialization process.[*] The commercialization of InnoGel™ was performed through a joint collaboration between NovoGEL and InterPharmaLink.

The InnoGel™ technology has been developed by NovoGEL, a spin-off company, which holds all rights to the InnoGel™ technology and acts as a licensor towards interested parties.

InterPharmaLink is a specialized healthcare management consulting firm that has the exclusive and worldwide mandate to commercialize the InnoGel™ technology. InterPharmaLink helps their clients optimize key resources along the value chain and create value added through product portfolio optimization, supply chain optimization and business development.

## Soft capsule market

About 100 billion soft capsules are produced throughout the world per year. Virtually all of this volume is manufactured by contract manufacturers and accounts for a market of about US$ 1.5 billion. Soft capsules are mainly applied in the industries of pharmaceuticals, health and nutrition, and cosmetics. The soft capsule market is dominated by two contract manufacturers: R.P. Scherer, the originator of the rotary die soft capsule manufacturing process and Banner Pharmacaps. The rest of the soft capsule market is served by several other companies.

Soft capsules are a means of packaging whereby the capsule content is encapsulated by a shell. The state of the art technology for the soft capsule shell is gelatin. The development of a non-animal alternative to gelatin has been a top priority in the soft capsule industry for many years. Several attempts to replace gelatin by non-animal material have been made already. But none of them have been overly successful. The InnoGel™ technology is a starch based gelatin replacement technology which has the clear potential to revolutionize the soft capsule market as it offers truly unique material properties and significant cost advantages versus gelatin.

---

[*] This case study was generously provided by Dr. Marc Müller, InterPharmaLink.

## InnoGel™ technology

The InnoGel™ technology is based on starch gel, an ordered material with a partly crystalline network structure. The network density can be adjusted by varying the composition and the physical treatment of the starch gel. It is the unique feature of the network structure that has lead experts to believe that the InnoGel™ technology can produce soft capsules for health and nutritional as well as for pharmaceutical products that offer major improvements to available technologies. These improvements manifest themselves in various strategic and financial benefits:

- Additional market potential due to suitability for vegetarians and cultures averse to animal sources (bovine or porcine);
- Increased value proposition vs. customers due to superior capsule properties and suitability as a lifecycle management tool for pharmaceutical products;
- Improved safety for end-users and reduced risk profile for customers due to elimination of BSE risks;
- Significantly lower raw material cost due to lower price of starch versus gelatin;
- Significantly lower process cost due to higher yield, less rejections, shorter process time, lower energy consumption and easier handling;
- Significantly lower packaging and logistic cost due to superior capsule properties.

## Commercialization process

The aspiration of the commercialization is to capture a maximum share of the value creation potential of the InnoGel™ technology. Thus, the successful commercialization of the InnoGel™ technology is performed along a clearly defined process. The commercialization process is structured in three major process steps:

Step 1: Define the basic conditions of the commercialization;
Step 2: Develop the strategy of the commercialization;
Step 3: Manage the out-licensing process.

### Step 1: Define the basic conditions of the commercialization

At the beginning, NovoGEL and InterPharmaLink agreed on the important conditions of the commercialization of the InnoGel™ technology with regard to confidentiality, timing and financials:

- Only non-confidential information could be disclosed to interested parties as the patent application is only published four months after the project starts.
- Only very limited financial and personal resources could be applied to the commercialization of InnoGel™, as NovoGEL is a start-up company with only limited financial capabilities.
- The first license should be granted within twelve months after project start in order to ensure the financial stability and future projects of NovoGEL.

In addition, both parties agreed on a collaboration agreement with clear incentives for both parties to fully exploit the value creation potential of the InnoGel™ technology and to perform the commercialization process in best time and at lowest cost.

### Step 2: Develop the strategy of the commercialization

The goal of the strategic planning of commercialization is to fully exploit the value creation potential of the InnoGel™ technology while considering the given conditions (i.e., tight schedule of commercialization and limited applicable resources). A successful commercialization strategy is based on a thorough analysis of the strategic landscape and addresses the strategic questions of where, how and when to compete.

The major soft capsule manufacturers were identified as the primary target group for commercialization. These contract manufacturers possess an extensive know-how and long-term experience in soft capsule manufacturing and have virtually all necessary equipment available to perform the technical evaluation, as well as the subsequent application development in best time. The most important selling arguments for contract manufacturers are cost saving potentials on the raw materials, as well as strategic aspects regarding BSE risks and issues. The soft capsule manufacturing process is mainly operated by contract manufacturers serving companies in the pharmaceutical, health and nutrition or cosmetics industry.

Thus, companies with considerable capsule volumes wanting to reduce or eliminate their dependency on contract manufacturers by re-integrating the soft capsule manufacturing into their in-house production facilities, have been evaluated as secondary target group.

The licensing-out of the InnoGel™ technology has been identified as the most promising approach for commercialization. As the InnoGel™ technology is still in the development stages and the future licensee will have to perform further development activities, a combined technical evaluation and option for licensing agreement is considered the most appropriate alternative. In order to ensure maximum know-how protection for licensee and licensor and preserve the exclusivity of the know-how, the out-licensing is done along the lines of a structured bidding process among interested parties.

The timeline of commercialization is set at the beginning of the project, meaning the first license should be granted within twelve months after project start. This early decision was mainly driven by the aspirations of the NovoGEL business plan.

Without these given constraints, a detailed assessment of the impact of the timeline on the exploitation of the value creation potential would have been the appropriate way to proceed. With an immediate commercialization the value creation potential for NovoGEL is clearly limited, as the InnoGel™ technology is an early development stage project with unproved realization guarantee. On the other hand, the risks for NovoGEL are clearly limited as well because the complete application development will be performed by the future licensee.

### Step 3: Manage the out-licensing process

In order to further develop and commercialize the InnoGel™ technology in a way that gives maximum protection of know-how to licensee and licensor, the out-licensing of InnoGel™ is done along the lines of a structured bidding process among the top global soft capsule manufacturers. The exclusive rights granted consist of the rights to perform an exclusive technical evaluation coupled with an option for subsequent licensing. In order to preserve the exclusivity of the know-how, the commercialization process incorporates the following basic principles:

- The exclusive technical evaluation is linked with the option for licensing. Therefore, the future licensee will have to sign a combined technical evaluation and option for licensing agreement prior to starting the exclusive technical evaluation phase.
- The detailed know-how for the exclusive technical evaluation (e.g., the recipe of the starch gel), as well as the process parameters will only be provided to the party signing the combined technical evaluation and option for licensing agreement.

The technical evaluation and option for licensing agreement incorporates the conditions of the exclusive technical evaluation phase as well as the conditions of a subsequent licensing agreement. Interested parties are offered the following conditions for an exclusive technical evaluation phase and subsequent licensing:

- The exclusive technical evaluation phase is limited to a three month period and is based on a detailed work plan describing the planned trials as well as the timelines to be met for the results. Both parties agree to 'target outcome results' in order to determine whether the technical evaluation is successful.
- Whether the technical evaluation is successful or not will be assessed by an independent committee on the basis of predetermined 'target outcome results'. Subsequently, the evaluating party has to decide whether it wants to exercise its option for licensing or not.
- All intellectual property rights and patents as well as results derived from activities during the technical evaluation phase shall belong to NovoGEL. In the case where the licensing option is exercised, the rights and results will be part of a subsequent license.

The decision with whom to enter into concrete negotiations to sign the combined technical evaluation and option for licensing agreement, is based on a set of qualitative and quantitative aspects; particularly the following:

- What timeline can be agreed upon and what trials are to be performed during the technical evaluation period?
- What technical evaluation fee is offered when signing the combined technical evaluation and option for licensing agreement?
- What down payment and/or exit fee is offered? A down payment is payable if the technical evaluation is successful and the evaluating party wants to exercise the option for licensing. An exit fee is payable if the technical evaluation is successful and the evaluating party does not want to exercise the option for licensing.
- What first and second milestone payments are offered? A first milestone payment is payable when the first health and nutritional product is on the market. A second milestone payment is payable when the first pharmaceutical product achieves regulatory approval.
- What royalties are offered? Royalties are payable based on the number of InnoGel™ capsules sold.

The decision with whom to enter into negotiations for signing the combined technical evaluation, and the option for the licensing agreement, is based on the attractiveness of the offers submitted by interested parties.

## Lessons learned

Lessons learned from the successful commercialization of InnoGel™ can be identified in the following three areas:

- Define the basic conditions and requirements of the commercialization with regard to timing and financials and set-up a detailed work plan;
- Analyze the market and develop a commercialization strategy that provides clear answers to the questions of where, how and when to compete and respect own resources;
- Set up a well structured out-licensing process that ensures the capture of a maximum share of the value of the technology for the licensor while preserving the exclusivity of know-how to the licensee. Conduct open and fair negotiations.

## Conclusions

The drug development pipeline is the engine that drives pharmaceutical companies. Market valuations of pharmaceutical companies are based on prospected new drug approvals and expected new drug revenues. What is feeding these new approvals is a healthy and steady discovery of new drug candidates. Given the inherently uncertain nature of research, pharmaceutical companies are introducing not only new technologies to widen the intake of new drug candidates (as described in chapter III), but also increasingly new management methods and techniques to make drug development more efficient.

These methods center around efficient and effective portfolio management and the use of external resources which can be accessed either via outsourcing or via collaborations. Typical forms of opening up the innovation process are:

- Outsourcing;
- Co-development and joint ventures;
- Crowdsourcing;
- Strategic alliances;
- In-licensing;
- Out-licensing;
- Spin-offs.

While overall pipeline management is becoming increasingly important, internationalization of research and development activities represents another challenge for pharmaceutical R&D managers that needs to be mastered for superior corporate performance. The opening up of the innovation process not only has a business but also a geographic component: Pharmaceutical innovation has become much more global than it was before. Drivers are these new collaborative forms but also new information and communication technology that has increased productivity in virtual R&D teams despite well-known support for trust and face-to-face demands.

In the following chapter we will describe how pharmaceutical companies are branching out globally to internationalize their R&D activities.

# V.    The Internationalization Challenge: Where to Get Access to Innovation

## Trends and Drivers of R&D Internationalization

As a science-driven endeavor, the pharmaceutical industry is inherently global. This is even truer for pharmaceutical companies originating in small countries, where high R&D costs can only be recouped by selling the resulting drug to a worldwide market. International trade statistics by the WTO (2002) illustrate the tremendous increase in international business over the past twenty years. For instance, the amount of worldwide merchandise exports has risen from about US$ 2 trillion to almost US$ 7 trillion between 1985 and 2000. Europe accounted for about 36 percent of the 2000 trade number (of which about 22 percent was intra-European trade), Asia about 28 percent, and the U.S. about 12 percent. Among the big movers is Asia, which almost doubled its worldwide share from 16 percent in 1980. China went up from about 1 percent to now 4 percent, and Korea, also increased from 1 percent to 3 percent. Africa is one of the losers in this picture, dropping from 6 percent to 2 percent by 2000.

Although many smaller multinationals that previously relied on centralized R&D now engage in sourcing technology from around the world, R&D internationalization during the 1980s and 1990s was largely driven by multinational companies. The pioneers of R&D internationalization are high-tech companies operating in small markets and with little R&D resources in their home country, as it is the case for ABB, Novartis and Roche (Switzerland), Philips (Netherlands) or Ericsson (Sweden). Swiss, Dutch and Belgian companies carried out more than 50 percent of their R&D outside their home country by the end of the 1980s. These companies increasingly conducted R&D in foreign research laboratories. Companies such as General Electric and General Motors in the USA, Toyota and Fujitsu in Japan, and DaimlerChrysler in Germany had large home markets and a substantial domestic R&D base, and hence had less pressure to internationalize their R&D activities. Only in recent years, increased competition from within and outside their industries forced these companies to source technological knowledge on a global scale.

Although the trend towards R&D internationalization had become apparent in the 1970s, it became a widespread phenomenon only as recently as in the late 1980s (Cantwell 1995). In the mid-1990s, the fifty largest R&D spenders worldwide accounted for a considerable share of total R&D input in each of the triad nations (33% in the US, 42% in Western Europe, and 57% in Japan), thus highlighting the importance of (international) R&D activities carried out by multinational companies (Gassmann and von Zedtwitz 1999). The significance of international R&D activities is even greater when indirect influence of these companies on small- and medium-sized enterprises is taken into account.

As early as 1986, Dutch and Swiss companies had more laboratories outside their home countries than within (Pearce, Singh 1990). Between 1985 and 1993, overseas investment in R&D by U.S. firms increased three times as fast as domestic R&D. In the US, overseas R&D expenses reached 10 percent of overall R&D investment, up from 6 percent in 1985 (National Science Board 1996). In the same period, the share of majority-owned foreign affiliates' R&D in the U.S. rose from 9 percent to over 15 percent (National Science Board 1996). In 1991, Japanese multinational companies conducted less than 5 percent of their R&D abroad (Buderi et al. 1991), but the recent establishment of Japanese laboratories in Europe and the U.S. has increased the significance of Japanese-based global R&D (see e.g., Dalton, Serapio 1995). By 1991, European companies performed about one third of their R&D outside of their home countries. More recent research shows that the trends of R&D internationalization in these three regions have been maintained (von Zedtwitz and Gassmann 2002).

The management of cross-border R&D activities is characterized by a significantly higher degree of complexity than local R&D management. The extra costs of international coordination must be balanced by synergy effects such as decreased time-to-market, improved effectiveness, and enhanced learning capabilities. Top corporate managers are confronted with the task of finding the optimal R&D organization based on the type of R&D activities, the present geographic dispersion of subsequent value-adding activities such as production and marketing, and the coordination between a multitude of contributors to the R&D process.

Nevertheless, the amount of international R&D activity is significant. Fig. 32 presents R&D investments of technology-intensive companies by rate of R&D internationalization and R&D-to-sales ratio. While many companies are still below 30 percent R&D internationalization, their total absolute overseas R&D investment is still very impressive given the large multiplier of their annual R&D budgets. Most highly internationalized R&D organizations are the results of merger and acquisition activity, as is the case for ABB, Royal Dutch/Shell, Mettler-Toledo, and others.

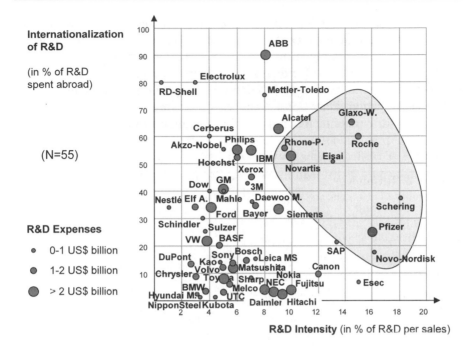

**Fig. 32.** Pharmaceutical firms have high degrees of R&D intensity and internationalization.

Pharmaceutical companies are characterized by a high R&D intensity (i.e. a high R&D-to-sales ratio). Many of the pharmaceutical companies included in Fig. 32 are in a variety of life science related businesses, and thus their R&D intensity increases even further (to an average of 20%) if sales only of ethical drugs are considered, which account for the lion's share of the R&D expenses. As pharmaceutical R&D is also relatively highly internationalized, most of the pharmaceutical firms are found in the top-right hand portion of the figure.

What drives R&D internationalization? Most factors are due to either science & technology-related issues or sales & output efficiency. Science & technology-related factors are concerned with R&D personnel qualification, know-how sourcing and regional infrastructure. These factors are largely outside the direct influence of R&D but necessary for its fundamental operations, such as the proximity to universities or the R&D environment. Proximity to markets and customers, improvements of image and collaborations are notable sales & output efficiency-related factors. Efficiency-related criteria focus on the costs of running and the critical mass of

R&D units, as well as efficient hand-over processes between R&D and other corporate functions. Direct cost advantages (such as the often publicized labor costs) rarely influence the internationalization of R&D, but other efficiency-oriented factors such as costs of coordination and transfer, and critical laboratory size do have an even bigger impact on international R&D organization. Direct costs may become more important in the coming years as the other factors improve in low labor cost countries.

**Table 6.** Reasons for locating R&D abroad.

| Science & Technology | Sales & Output Efficiency |
|---|---|
| Availability of scientists and engineers | Smooth hand-over with local marketing and sales organization |
| Tapping into local scientific community | |
| Proximity to universities | Easier coordination with local hospitals during the clinical phases |
| Recruiting local talent | |
| Better R&D environment | Compliance with local regulatory requirements |
| Higher quality of life | |
| Lower R&D costs | 24-h-Laboratories |
| Higher acceptance for pharmaceutical research | 'Good citizen' argument |
| | Local content rules |
| | Protectionist barriers |
| | Tax optimization |

Political and socio-cultural factors such as local content rules, technology acceptance and public approval times, all play an important role in locating R&D abroad. Protectionist, legal and cultural constraints imposed by national governments, however, often require a company to establish local R&D units. R&D-external forces such as a business unit's striving for autonomy and the build-up of local competence alters the original mission of a local R&D unit. This evolution may take place unbeknownst to headquarters, particularly in strongly decentralized companies.

In the pharmaceutical industry, mergers and acquisitions have significantly contributed to the internationalization of R&D, particularly with recent cross-border mergers. Subsequent cost reduction programs eliminated R&D units in the combined company, but since both domestic and foreign units were closed down, this had little effect on their new extent of R&D internationalization. Rather, we observed a centralization of R&D in certain internationally leading regions of innovation (centers of excellence). However, mergers are rarely driven by scientific or technological reasons. Access to new markets and economies-of-scale effects are primary drivers for mergers. Nevertheless, the resulting R&D conglomerate has to live and cope with a new more international organization.

The development of local products requires the early involvement of market and customer application know-how, which is more likely to be found in regional business units. Companies with local R&D exhibit an inclination towards over-emphasizing different local market specification in order to support local autonomy and independence from the parent company. Host country restrictions, such as local content requirements, tolls, import quota, and fulfillment of standards, can attract R&D into key market countries (pull regulations). On the other hand, home country restrictions may induce companies to move R&D abroad (push regulations): European regulations caused biotechnology R&D to be transferred to the US. In addition, external factors have had a great impact on the dispersion of R&D sites.

The case for R&D internationalization is not unanimous. Besides the ubiquitous cost argument, foreign R&D units are more difficult to manage, and control, and may be less efficient due to missed scale effects. The following table summarizes some of the most cited arguments against international R&D.

**Table 7.** Barriers to R&D internationalization.

| Factors in support of central R&D | Obstacles to international R&D |
|---|---|
| Economies of scale (critical size) | Immobility of top-class personnel |
| Synergy effects | Critical mass (for start-ups) |
| Higher career potential | Redundant development |
| Minimal R&D costs and development time | Language and cultural differences |
| | Effective communication difficult |
| Better control over research results | Much of scientific and technical information worldwide available by Internet |
| Communication intensity | |
| Legal protection | Specific know-how easily lost when support not present |
| Global product standards | |
| Common R&D culture | Political risks in target country |
| Harmonization of regulatory environment | Establishment and running costs |
| | No wage advantages in triad nations |
| Improved information and communication technologies | Coordination and information costs |

## Primary Locations of Pharmaceutical R&D around the World

As the pharmaceutical R&D pipeline is one of the key indicators for future blockbuster drugs and thus revenues, stock prices fluctuate with good or bad news emanating from the R&D pipeline. Investor pressure has led pharmaceutical companies to document their R&D activities comparatively well. Let us consider, for example, the international R&D network of Novartis.

In early 2003, Novartis had 67 drug candidates in clinical development. About 3,000 scientists worked in 10 research centers worldwide in a number of therapeutic areas. Only 1,400 of them are employed in research centers in Switzerland, along with a comparable number in pre-clinical and clinical development (see also Zeller 2001). More than half of the R&D workforce is located outside Switzerland (see Fig. 33). A more detailed overview of Novartis' global R&D activities today is provided later on in chapter VI.

A study of 1,021 R&D sites across various industries (including automotive, engineering, electrical, IT, software, food, chemical and pharmaceutical companies) produced the following overall results concerning international R&D locations (von Zedtwitz and Gassmann 2002):

- R&D is concentrated in the Triad regions of Europe, the United States, Japan, as well as major regional centers in South Korea, Singapore and other emerging economies along the Pacific Rim, such as China. Research is more concentrated than development. Over seventy percent (73.2%) of all research sites are located in the five regions of the Northeastern USA (New Jersey, New York, Massachusetts), California, the United Kingdom, Western Continental Europe (in particular Germany), and the Far East (Japan, South Korea). The trend of research concentration is even more apparent when only foreign research locations are considered: 87.4 percent operate in the Triad.
- Although the main regional centers for development largely coincide with the regional centers for research, development is more evenly distributed among European countries and the Northeastern United States, and extends into Southeast Asia, Australia, Africa, and South America. Only slightly more than half (53.4%) of all development sites are located in the eight most development-intensive countries. Development sites from 19 countries must be considered in order to account for a similar share in worldwide development (74.2%) as the top eight countries in research (73.2%).

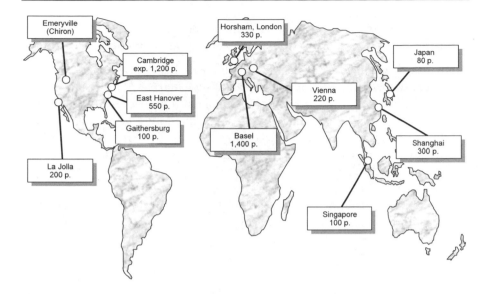

**Fig. 33.** The research network of Novartis in 2006.

Moreover, research and development sites of the same company are not necessarily co-located. For instance, AstraZeneca operates research as well as development units in the United States. A research unit in Waltham, Massachusetts focuses on infectious diseases. Since there is no complementary development in the US, their research findings are transferred to a development laboratory in Sweden. The 1990s have seen an effort of many large companies to consolidate their activities in order to realize synergy and coordination potential in international R&D. Transnational R&D projects are managed more easily if the R&D network consists of competence centers such as is the case for Roche or Novartis, given that complementary competencies are provided locally. With increasing complementarities of resources, competencies, and knowledge bases, as well as the division of labor and specialization of work, synergy potentials in R&D projects can be exploited.

Fig. 34 shows a subset of 193 pharmaceutical R&D laboratories of the 1,021 R&D locations studied earlier. It includes R&D locations of AHP, AstraZeneca, Boehringer Ingelheim, Eli Lilly, Eisai, Glaxo Wellcome, Pfizer, Novartis, Novo Nordisk, Roche, Schering, and Yamanouchi. The distribution of these R&D sites shows a similar pattern to the overall set but differs in the following observations:

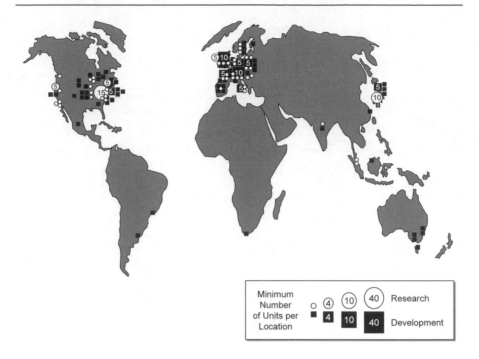

**Fig. 34.** Locations of 193 R&D labs of 12 pharmaceutical firms (data collected from 1997-2003).

- In the US, R&D is focused more on the North-East and Mid-West; the relative importance of the Pacific Coast has declined;
- In Europe, R&D is more evenly distributed. Overall, Europe seems to host a greater share of development sites compared to the US;
- There are very few R&D laboratories (only 15) outside the Triad regions.

Given this data, the pharmaceutical industry is one of the most internationalized in terms of R&D locations, with one foreign R&D lab for every domestic lab. Pharmaceutical companies also seem to internationalize research as fast as development (albeit for different reasons). Most other industries tend to keep research at home and localize development. Although not obvious from location data alone, pharmaceutical companies also tend to organize R&D as competence-based networks, as opposed to R&D hubs (e.g., automotive and chemicals), polycentric networks (e.g., local market-dependent companies such as Royal Dutch/Shell) or centralized R&D (e.g., dominant design industries). In competence-based R&D networks, each R&D node has a clearly defined competence – and responsibility! –

which it brings into the network of other R&D centers. The coordination and management of such R&D networks is more demanding and costly than rather centralized and directive R&D hubs, or the laissez-faire style of polycentric R&D networks. As a consequence, pharmaceutical companies (and many electrical and IT companies, who also favor this R&D organization) try to coordinate R&D activities across multiple levels, including the deployment of transnational project teams, platform management, informal as well as formal network techniques. The next chapter illustrates the new opportunities arising for pharmaceutical companies to conduct (parts of) their R&D in China.

# New Opportunities for Drug Development in China

## The pharma context in China

Since the reform from a planned to a market economy started in the late 1970s, China GDP has grown at an average 8 percent per annum, and in excess of 10 percent in the 2000s. A country of more than 1.3 billion people, its economy currently is the size of Germany with a GDP of about US$ 2.7 trillion.

Most of China is still a developing country, which means relatively little attention to healthcare and the pharmaceutical industry in general. Despite limited short-term returns, major pharmaceutical companies pursue aggressive growth strategies and try to benefit from the Chinese market in the longer term. They invest in the sourcing of active ingredients, research and development, and the production and selling of generic and proprietary drugs. In this context, administrative hurdles, low healthcare spending, the lack of intellectual property protection and the poor distribution network infrastructure remain the biggest challenges.

Still, it is expected that China's share of the global pharmaceutical market will increase from about US$ 6 billion in 2002 to an estimated US$ 24 billion by the end of 2010. China has the world's fastest-growing over-the-counter (OTC) drug market and is now the second largest pharmaceutical chemical producer. China's one-child policy leads to wealth being distributed among fewer children and family members, which means that more earnings are disposable for life-style and health-related products. Improved living conditions further mean that China's population is aging fast, with the share of the population aged 65 or older to double to about 13 percent by 2025. Furthermore, as China westernizes, its disease profile will become more and more comparable with the Western world, including afflictions such as hypertension, cancer, diabetes, AIDS, etc., for which multinational companies already have developed drugs and therapies.

## Chinese pharma

The Chinese pharmaceutical market for chemical or small-molecule medicines (i.e. not including herbal medicines or traditional Chinese medicines) is largely a generic market, with a modest (but increasing) share taken by innovative patented medicines. In 2003, there were approximately 6,800 Chinese pharmaceutical companies, of which 5,000 produced medicines (small-molecule generics and biotech products) and the remainder were involved in pharmaceutical-related activities such as packaging and equipment supply (Webber 2005). It is expected that compliance with international GMP (good manufacturing process) will weed out about half of the more than these 6,800 drug companies operating in China. About 1,700 of these are foreign investments and less than 1,000 are GMP-certified. More than 1,350 of the manufacturing drug companies are producers of raw materials (Wang and von Zedtwitz, 2005).

Chinese manufacturers are very strong in their ability to copy foreign drugs, sometimes selling them under the foreign label. Almost 99 percent of the 3,000 pharmaceutical products manufactured in China are copies of foreign products, either legal generics or illegal counterfeits. Webber (2005) states to many Chinese companies, even the very term 'R&D' has a different meaning, usually referring to the production of additional *generic* products particularly for China – in terms of strengths, dosage forms and even specific compounds.

Thus, the Chinese market is dominated by generic drugs. In 2003, unbranded generics (products marketed under the generic name of their active ingredient) commanded 19 percent of the overall market. Original and licensed brands represented a combined 19 percent (Brueckner et al. 2005). Other products – mainly comprising branded generics, copycat products and products without licensing agreements – account for more than 60 percent of the market.

Chemical products account for around 70 percent of the pharmaceutical market in China. Biopharmaceuticals make up 7 percent. But besides the ethical, mostly foreign-dominated drug market, more than 8,000 (including different dosage forms) traditional Chinese medicines (TCM) are manufactured and sold. TCM (accounting for 24 percent) posts above-market growth and are particularly strong in rural areas.

TCM have played an important role in health care in Chinese and other oriental cultures for thousands of years. In 2001, it was reported that there were 1,036 TCM manufacturers in 31 provinces, although many Chinese pharmaceutical companies include a few TCM products in their portfolios.

TCM provide a huge opportunity for foreign and domestic innovation alike. The Chinese Government promotes TCMs and a number of government departments are guiding the TCM industry's attempts to modernize. According to Webber (2005), the Chinese authorities have identified two tracks for developing TCM R&D. The first is through purification and standardization to meet global standards and remove impurities such as pesticides and heavy metals. The second track is to utilize TCM as a starting point for producing *novel* medicines. This may be through the identification and purification of the active element(s) (often complex molecules) or the discovery and development of small molecules which mimic the activity of the original TCM. It has been claimed that about 140 new drugs have originated directly or indirectly from Chinese medicinal plants by means of modern scientific methods (Liu and Xiao 2002).

The Chinese government has also set clear focus on certain areas of biotech research. In particular, it aims to become a leader in genomics research. In 1998, the Ministry of Science and Technology established the Chinese National Human Genome Centre based in Beijing and Shanghai, and the Beijing Institute of Genomics, as centers of excellence for genome sequencing and analysis, thus enabling China to join the International Human Genome Sequencing Consortium in 1999, in which China played a significant part. China now is on par with major international research leaders in areas such as gene mapping, transgenic technology for animals and plants, gene therapy technology, stem cell research, gene chips and gene research of some major diseases (Webber 2005). The country has a number of world-class scientific biomedical institutions – the North and South Genome Centers, The Institute of Materia Medica, Tsinghua and Beijing Universities, for example. China also has some 200 research institutes for biotechnology and more than 30 of the 150 key state laboratories in biopharmaceutical-related areas.

In China, the domestic pharmaceutical research and development environment is dominated by universities and scientific institutes rather than pharmaceutical enterprises. The industrialization of pharmaceutical research and biotechnology still lags behind the Western world, with relatively few biotech companies in existence. Local companies already have substantial assets and knowledge in generics manufacture and low-cost, increasingly high-quality operations. It is easy to envisage these companies becoming the world's principal suppliers of quality generic products. The question addressed here is whether some of them could develop innovative R&D and evolve into research-based pharmaceutical companies (Webber 2005). Closing the gap to the international standards is much harder in highly innovative fields with a risk of failure, such as the identification and validation of disease targets. Hence, domestic private enterprises are hesitating to research new drugs on their own. As a consequence, domestic firms hold only 3 percent of the intellectual property rights to all chemical drugs on the Chinese market (Chen 2004). According to the State Food and Drug Administration of China, the remaining 97 percent are legal imitations of imported drugs.

## Foreign pharma in China

Around 60 percent of the nearly 900 new small molecule chemical entities introduced as drugs worldwide during the last 20 years can be traced back to natural products (Newman et al. 2003). One impressive example is one of the most successful and best-selling drug ever: Lipitor with annual sales of over US$ 13 billion, which belongs to the compound class named statins first discovered in natural sources. China is still a fairly unexploited resource of such natural products. The wealth of TCM is only an indication of what might be so far have been undiscovered for Western pharmaceutical research. China-based innovations include Artemisinin, invented in China using sweet wormwood and hailed as a miracle malaria drug, Sobuzoxan, an anti-tumor drug, and Huperzine A (HupA), a novel alkaloid isolated from a Chinese medicinal herb, which improves memory deficiencies in Alzheimer patients.

In the past few years, there has been a sharp rise in foreign investment in research and development (R&D) in China, in part to access the natural resource base in China, and in part to tap into an increasingly large body of medical researchers and pharmaceutical scientists. Last but not least, China is also an attractive base for clinical research, given that there were more than 300,000 hospitals and healthcare facilities in China in 2003 (compare Chinese Ministry of Health).

Local R&D presence usually begins with R&D collaborations. GlaxoSmithKline (GSK), for instance, has invested over US$ 10 million in co-operative R&D with Chinese research institutions since the mid-1990s. Novartis has a collaboration with the Shanghai Institute of Materia Medica (SIMM), with the objective of isolating compounds from Chinese medicinal plants for Novartis to further screen and identify lead compounds. After an initial phase and US$ 2 million in funding, training and equipment, SIMM had by 2004 isolated more than 1,800 compounds from natural herbs covering immunology, oncology, diabetes and the central nervous system. With additional funding, SIMM was expected to isolate a further 1,500 compounds for Novartis over the next three years.

A number of other foreign pharmaceutical companies have started R&D laboratories in China for several years (see Table 8).

**Table 8.** Foreign pharmaceutical R&D centers in China.

| Year | MNC | Name | Location | Investment | Objective |
|------|-----|------|----------|------------|-----------|
| 2001 | Servier | Servier (Beijing) R&D Center | Beijing | n/a | Develop potential value for TCM |
| 2002 | Novo Nordisk | Novo Nordisk (China) R&D Center | Beijing | n/a | General biotech research |
| 2003 | Astra-Zeneca | East-Asia Clinical Research Center | Shanghai | First year: US$ 4 million | Clinical research Collaboration with Health & Medical Institute in China Localize therapeutic methods |
| 2003 | Eli Lilly | Shanghai Chem Explorer Co Ltd. | Shanghai | All funds supplied by Eli Lilly, > 100 scientists | Combining different kinds of organic substance for new drugs |
| 2004 | Roche | China R&D Center | Shanghai | First year several million, 50 scientists | Phase I: Chemical drugs; analyzing compound structures Phase II: TCM & genetic engineering |
| 2004 | GSK | n/a | Tianjin | 16 scientists | Develop 20 new OTC products in next 3 years |
| 2004 | J&J | n/a | Shanghai | n/a | Develop medications suitable for Chinese and Asians |
| 2005 | Pfizer | n/a | Shanghai | US$ 25 million | Trial protocol design and assessment |
| 2006 | Novartis | Novartis Institutes for BioMedical Research | Shanghai | US$ 100 million, 400 scientists | Cancer & infectious diseases |

Source: SMIE Medicine Information and own research

In 1997, Novozymes opened an R&D center in the Zhongguancun Science Park in Beijing. Costing EUR 10 million, the facility is involved in the customized development of enzymes and processes for the Chinese market. Roche has opened a new R&D center for 40 chemists in the Zhangjiang High-Tech Park and established R&D alliances with the state-owned genomics centers in Shanghai and Beijing, to conduct research in the genetic predisposition to diseases such as diabetes and Alzheimer's. Local R&D enables foreign pharma companies to enter into a dialogue with authorities and opinion leaders in the country, which they expect to boost business in China. In July 2004, GlaxoSmithKline China set up an OTC (over-the-counter) medicines R&D center at Tianjin Smith Kline & French Laboratories, a joint venture funded by GlaxoSmithKline. Its aim is to excel in creating innovative science-based products to meet consumer needs and support the joint venture's vision of becoming the premier OTC company in China. Pfizer set up an R&D center in Shanghai focusing on developing trial protocol design and assessment of trial results. Their center seems to be more development focused rather than basic research oriented. Novartis built a US$ 100 million drug discovery research center in Shanghai in 2006. The research facility, which will have about 400 scientists by 2008, will focus initially on discovering medicines to treat cancers caused by infections, which make up a considerable proportion of the can-

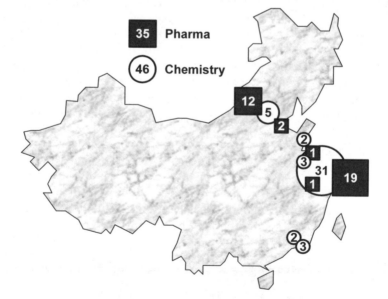

**Fig. 35.** Locations of foreign pharmaceutical and chemical R&D centers in China (data as of 2006).

cer cases diagnosed in China. Many pharmaceutical companies, such as Sanofi-Aventis and others, are considering R&D in China. Some smaller biotech firms have already started local R&D in China, for instance BiColl in Shanghai. For the time being, pharma research has focused on Shanghai and Beijing (see Fig. 35), while other industries have already explored locations in second-tier cities and interior China.

It is important to note that R&D in China is a trend in the beginning. Many more R&D collaborations and institutes will be set up to make use of the vast gene pool in China (for clinical trials), the increasing level of scientific and technical capabilities in pharmaceutical research, or the still untapped and underresearched substances – any of which could be the source for the next blockbuster. The question is whether economic growth coupled with the shaping of a positive environment will encourage increasing investment into innovative pharmaceutical R&D in China (Webber 2005). The global pharma companies are well advised to explore the China option carefully and systematically, given the dangers involved, but certainly they are advised to take this opportunity seriously. The next chapters illustrate some typical problems in international R&D and related management techniques.

## Three Principal Problems of Dispersed R&D

Once companies internationalize their business, the question sooner or later is raised when R&D and product development should follow, where it should be located, and how this should be done. We have already pointed out that this trend towards R&D internationalization comes with caveats and difficulties at the strategic and organizational level. But it is at the team level where dispersion of R&D really does the greatest damage.

When people and teams are geographically dispersed, problems of coordination and communication become more important. In international R&D, the most significant problems have been identified as:

1. Lack of face-to-face time
2. Cultural differences
3. Lack of trust

### Problem 1: Lack of face-to-face time

People are more creative when they can interact with colleagues with whom they can trust, bounce ideas off, and explain themselves in a variety of ways. In dispersed teams, access and contact to colleagues is restricted, communication is often asynchronous and limited to information and communication technologies, such as the telephone. This is a major problem particularly in the early phases of R&D, when formal creativity techniques such as brainstorming or informal ones such as water cooler discussions are key ingredients to finding effective solutions. Information and communication technologies are also good for the exchange of explicit, data-driven information only, but fail at providing communication that is rich in experience in multiple communication dimensions, such as interactive shared-access graphics, three-dimensionality, haptic and sensory information, etc.

Lack of face time can already inhibit R&D work in non-international settings. For instance, after a large pharmaceutical company redesigned one of their R&D centers, management decided it would be a good idea to allow their scientists to work longer in their labs, ordering the cafeterias on each lab floor to provide lunch-bags for anyone who wished. As a positive side effect, the cafeterias could be made smaller as it had to accommodate fewer people. Consequently, scientists picked up their lunches, retreated to their benches and missed out on the opportunity to share their insights informally over lunch. When this became apparent, management abolished the lunch-bag option. Additionally, they closed most lab floor cafeterias and opened a large central cafeteria on a single floor. Scientists now meet colleagues and peers from different departments and labs, improving informal exchange of knowledge and information.

## Problem 2: Cultural differences

It is all too obvious that we are different, and regional commonalities of these differences are often denoted by culture. There are two important notions for international R&D work in culture:

1. Cultural differences making cooperation more difficult.
2. Different cultures and their relation to innovation and creativity.

The first source of problems has been described by Hofstede (1980) in his work on cultural distances between countries. Surveying 88,000 IBM employees, he arrived at five cultural dimensions that explained different behavioral preferences (see Fig. 36). Although some of us may share the same perception of, for example, the importance of hierarchy and ranks, we may have a very different opinion when it comes to values on individualism or collectivism. Thus we all differ from each other, but in different ways. This makes managing multi-cultural teams not particularly easy.

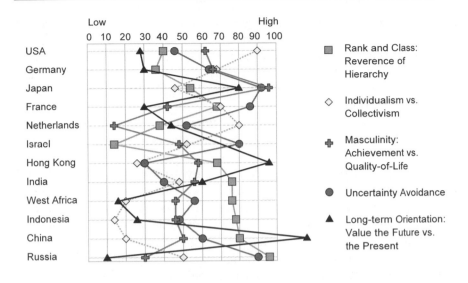

**Fig. 36.** Cultural differences among countries (adapted from Hofstede 1980).

The second source of problems has been research by Shane (1992 and 1993), who studied the rate of invention by people from 33 different nations. He found that people from individualistic and non-hierarchical societies are more inventive (measured in patents per capita) than other societies. By implication, some societies may have a cultural comparative advantage in inventiveness, and corporations should consider establishing R&D centers in these countries. Also, it means that companies may not be able to increase the rates of innovation simply by increasing the amount of money spent on R&D in a given country. Shane also found that per capita income was more important than industrial structure in determining national rates of innovation, indicating that as nations become wealthier, they also become more innovative. Shane's findings certainly have strong implications for the selection of individuals in certain phases of R&D and innovation work, as well as consideration of the R&D mission when choosing a location for a new R&D site.

## Problem 3: Lack of trust

Trust is a vital ingredient in R&D work where intellectual property is often not yet claimed or clearly assigned. Lack of trust leads to secrecy, keeping potentially good ideas to oneself, and consequently to unexploited opportunities of innovation. There are many ways to build trust in teams, but separating individual team members is certainly not one of them. Through physical distance, individuals cannot communicate as often and as well as they used to, they do not share common work space or referential frameworks, and they may become absorbed more in the local R&D setting rather than as feeling part of the international R&D project. Lack of trust is a great barrier to innovation.

How can transnational R&D teams counteract the loss of trust? First of all, it is difficult enough to establish trust in any team. This is, however, a precondition for any high-performing team. The four stages of group development start with 'forming', followed by 'storming', 'norming', and eventually 'performing' (see e.g., West 1998). The 'forming' stage is critically dependent on good communication, informal get-togethers, and creating a unique project spirit. This is difficult to achieve at a distance for truly innovative projects, and only possible in distance teams if scientific or technical domains provide a common bracket and work interdependencies are minimal (see e.g., Gassmann and von Zedtwitz 2003).

Thus, even the most transnational R&D team will have to resort to travel, at least for some of its members. Typically, a kick-off meeting, which should last at least a day and better if it allows social time for a dinner, starts the actual project work. Trust can be built here, or at least a working relationship can be established. Once the team disperses again, communication will be limited to information and communication tech-

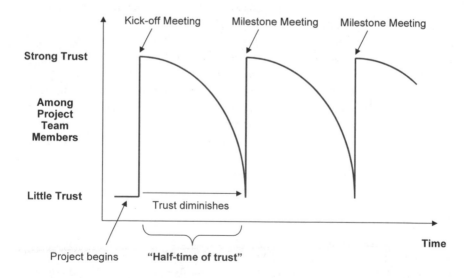

**Fig. 37.** Half-time of trust: E-mail is not enough in coordinating a high-performance team.

nologies, which are good for exchanging explicit information but inappropriate for establishing a tacit communication dimension. Thus, trust is likely to diminish, and a new meeting must take place (e.g., a milestone meeting or review) to allow time for building mutual respect and confidence (see Fig. 37 for a simplified representation of this scheme).

How much time that should be allowed to pass is unclear. De Meyer (1991) coined the term 'half-time of trust' to denote the period of time in which trust is halved. R&D managers in the engineering and automotive industries indicated that two to three full-team meetings per year are appropriate to maintain a common team spirit. This must be supported by more frequent visits to each subteam by the overall team manager or project integrator. Other, more subtle means of building common team brackets, such as a company-wide recognition like a 'Golden Badge' or 'High Risk' team, may sustain team identity, and certainly involves the support of top management.

## Conclusions

R&D organizations have developed from centralized and geographically confined towards distributed and open structures. Some of the most frequent challenges that arise during R&D internationalization cover the following fundamental dilemmas:

- Local versus global;
- Process versus hierarchy;
- Control versus collaborative R&D;
- Open versus closed innovation;
- Creativity versus discipline;
- Face to face versus information and communication technologies;
- Short-term versus long-term.

Dilemmas are not negative per se. To the contrary, in a dilemma both alternative courses of action are equally valuable. The various approaches to managing these dilemmas – including those that attempt to eliminate them altogether – have given rise to an impressive body of know-how among R&D managers and R&D scientists. However, one issue remains constant: Looking ten years ahead, regardless of the rapid evolution of modern technologies, new organizational concepts and even more efficient tools, the individual and teams will remain at the core of international management of innovation.

The key lessons learned for managing global R&D in the pharmaceutical industry can be classified as follows:

- Localization of management resources;
- Flat and flexible organizations;
- Introduction of local culture of innovation and know-how;
- Challenging projects coupled with bottom-up creativity;
- Personal interactions more important in decentralized R&D;
- Synchronization of international drug development by means of transnational project management in order to shorten R&D cycles;
- Worldwide integrated R&D data management;
- Acquisition of external ideas and projects as important as internal R&D;
- International teams require new organizations;
- Manage platforms, not individual R&D projects;
- Foster networking and collaboration.

In conclusion, the pharmaceutical industry is one of the most advanced in terms of R&D internationalization, and one of the most specific when it comes to regulation and significance of science and technology. R&D management is a key ingredient to success, and the high stakes of the drug approval and medical safety have made the pharmaceutical innovation pipeline one of the best understood R&D engines. However, there is still untapped potential to improve this engine with new technologies, new managerial approaches, and new scientific talent drawn from countries around the world.

# VI.  Management Answers to Pharmaceutical R&D Challenges

## Managing R&D Organization at Roche

Roche's research is based on a distinctive innovation model and a clear strategy in which partnerships play a key role. Apart from Roche's own powerful in-house research organization, the pharmaceuticals division's R&D network also includes Genentech and Chugai, which function as largely independent research satellites. In addition, Roche has opt-in rights to the programs of external development organizations it has created, such as BioXell, set up in 2002, and Basilea Pharmaceutica. This is a further source of promising compounds for the company's product pipeline. Including several research related agreements with other companies, Roche ranks among the industry leaders in terms of licensing. In total, the Roche Group owns 166 patents (Reuters 2002).

As of January 2003, Roche has been pursuing 135 pharmaceutical research projects in-house (see Table 9). In 2002, 12 new molecular entities entered phase 0, and seven entered phase I clinical testing. The pharmaceuticals division currently has 65 new molecular entities in its development pipeline. This includes opt-in opportunities (9), potential new medicines that Genentech will develop (6) and Chugai projects (10). Roche has the right to license-in any projects for which Chugai seeks a partner outside

**Table 9.** R&D pipeline of Roche in January 2003.

| Area of Focus | Number of Projects |
|---|---|
| Central nervous system | 24 |
| Genitourinary diseases | 9 |
| Inflammatory diseases | 17 |
| Metabolic diseases | 30 |
| Oncology | 37 |
| Vascular diseases | 8 |
| Virology | 10 |
| **Total** | **135** |

Japan and South Korea. The increased number of promising new molecular entities compared with 2001 is a result of structural adjustments in the pharmaceutical R&D organization. The number of projects in phase II development has increased significantly during the past two years. The seamless R&D process which Roche has established in recent years promotes better decision-making and thus contributes to creating greater future value. Ongoing initiatives are concentrating on further optimizing productivity, with the focus more on the value generated by each project than on quantity. Progress has been achieved by implementing a number of tools for compound selection and profiling at the early research stage. These have been harmonized across all research centers.

At Roche, the research and development organizations are separated and organized in different ways. On the one hand, research is performed at four major research sites (see Table 10); each site acts as a center of excellence for a certain disease area. On the other hand, development is globally coordinated with the project leaders located in different areas, mainly at the same sites as the research activities.

Additionally, research and development have different organizational structures. Research is organized to allow innovation and maintain a certain degree of freedom necessary for the creativity of scientists in research. Development is focused on the management task of bringing drug candidates to market as quickly and efficiently as possible.

The present geographical research site configuration is in place mainly for historical reasons. The Basel site evolved from Roche's classical research areas such as bacteriology, central nervous system and cardiovascular disease. Metabolic disease and autoimmune disease were established from the beginning in the US.

**Table 10.** R&D sites and designated research areas at Roche in 2003.

| Sites | Research Areas |
|---|---|
| Basel, Switzerland | Metabolic disorders |
| | Central nervous system |
| | Vascular disease |
| Nutley, USA | Metabolic disorders |
| | Oncology |
| | Vascular disease |
| Palo Alto, USA | Central nervous system |
| | Inflammatory disease/bone |
| | Genitourinary disease |
| | Viral disease |
| Penzberg, Germany | Oncology |

Each center has a certain technology in which it excels and offers this technology as a service to the other centers. Nutley, for example, has extensive knowledge in the genomics area through close links with specialized biotechnology companies such as Millennium.

Development is globally coordinated with a Project Development Meeting responsible for the entire steering of drug development. Projects are developed according to the requirements of the key countries of market interest which are the USA, Japan and the major European markets. An International Project Team is the key organizational group for developing prescription medicines. An international project manager leading the International Project Team is usually located at the site where most of the research leading to the development project takes place.

## Managing R&D Strategy at Schering

Schering AG (acquired by its German rival Bayer in 2007) used to have an R&D management approach characterized by several key features which were established to respond to the business requirements of fast, synchronized global drug development and market entry, to the harmonization of international regulatory requirements, and to rescue limitations in R&D which are a consequence of cost increases due to increased regulatory requirements (see e.g., Müller (2000) of Project Coordination at Schering).

Rather than a clear-cut centralized organization with direct power over all R&D facilities, a decentralized organization coordinated by corporate management processes and a strong International Project Management was chosen. This method was expected to best combine global R&D capabilities and flexible responses to meet local needs.

Strategic R&D management is overseen at board level by the Portfolio Board and includes the setting of Schering's R&D strategy, decisions on major R&D collaborations, decisions on initiation and start of Phase III development projects, and yearly prioritization as well as continuous adjustments of prioritization for the entire portfolio of development projects (Fig. 38). Portfolio Board decisions concerning research are operationalized by the International Research Management Conference (chaired by the Executive Board Member of R&D), which takes care of research budget setting and control, all decisions concerning research projects and research cooperations (below Portfolio Board-level), and periodical project reviews.

Portfolio Board-decisions concerning development projects are operationalized by the International Development Team, chaired by the head of

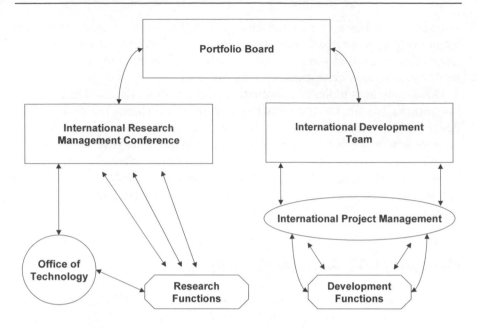

**Fig. 38.** Coordination of pharmaceutical R&D management at Schering.

International Project Management and represent all major resource-holders in international R&D. The International Development Team closely inter-acts with International Project Management and its responsibilities cover development budget planning and control, all operational decisions con-cerning development projects, and all operational issues concerning the international R&D organization and management processes in R&D. The International Development Team also monitors the composition and per-formance of the International Project Teams.

Disciplinary and functional reporting lines are dissociated in many parts of the R&D organization. While all headquarters' R&D function report directly to the Executive Board Member of R&D, functions located in the affiliates discipline report to the local hierarchy. Functional reporting, however, in the case of research, is a task for the Executive Board Member of R&D and, in the case of development, for the International Develop-ment Team.

Core members of the International Project Teams disciplinary report to their home-based and functionally report to their respective international project manager.

Proposals for new R&D projects can come from all parts of the organi-zation. They are, however, in the case of research projects, subject to formal proposal-agreement processes, organized by the International Research Management Conference, or, in the case of development projects, subject to formats and processes established by International Project Management. Decisions on new development projects are recommended by the International Development Team and made by the Portfolio Board. Local projects are possible, but no R&D project may be conducted without a decision from either the International Research Management Conference (research) or the International Development Team/Portfolio Board (development), and all milestone decisions are subject to the respective corporate processes.

1. International research coordination below the level of the International Research Management Conference (i.e., on project/program level) is done by international research project groups.
2. International development coordination is the responsibility of International Project Management, supported by coordinators in the affiliates.

Worldwide networking with academic and commercial R&D institutes and, search activities for project and product opportunities, are supported strategically and have become progressively important and complex. Therefore, an Office of Technology (a total of 15 employees, based in Berlin, USA and Japan) was established, which conducts all scientific intelligence, networking and search activities on behalf of the Strategic Business Units and of the R&D functions. The Office of Technology defines areas of interest with its partners in the R&D organization, and within these areas of interest proactively provides the R&D organization with scientific intelligence and cooperation opportunities. An international management process has been established, along which the Office of Technology interfaces with the R&D organization, with Corporate Licensing and the decision-making bodies. After identification of concrete cooperation opportunities, the Office of Technology runs the initial negotiations and, after the contracts have been signed, provides also contract management services.

## Managing the Research-to-Development Handover at Roche

Time-to-market is extremely important in breakthrough pharmaceuticals: The first in the market captures 40 to 60 percent of the market, and the second only around 15 percent. Coming in behind third oftentimes means a negative business.

Roche therefore puts great emphasis on development speed. "Projects first, budgets second", said Roche's former Head of R&D Controlling, Alfons Wunschheim. Delaying market introduction of a blockbuster drug by two months not only involves the risk that a competitor seizes significant market share, it also means a net loss of US$ 100 million, or almost US$ 2 million a day.

In research, integrated disease units (IDUs) have been formed which have all the necessary functions and technologies to bring projects to a state where they can be handed over to development. The IDUs have a great deal of autonomy over how they achieve the goals that are set by the Research Board. Development candidates must be active, efficient, and safe. These requirements have been tested in animals.

The Research Board selects prospective development candidates and proposes them to the Product Development Board. Critical parameters are human compatibility, a medical need, and a business case. Not all projects can be proposed, and some projects are returned to research for later consideration or rework. The earlier a no-go decision can be taken the better, since extending ill-fated research projects only wastes money (Fig. 39).

The Product Development Board evaluates the development candidates proposed by the Research Board. Some of the candidates are accepted, others are turned away. Until recently, these diverted candidates have been

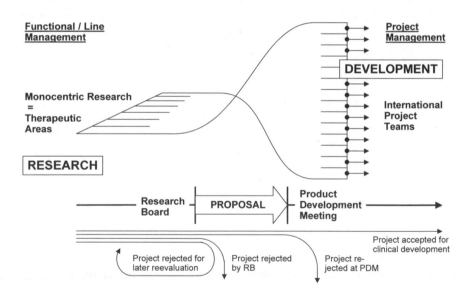

Source: von Zedtwitz (1999)

**Fig. 39.** Project handover between research and development at Roche.

divested. It is currently under discussion whether Roche should sell them to competing pharmaceutical companies. Accepted development candidates, however, enter the International Drug Development System (IDDS) which guides them through the various clinical and regulatory development stages.

Each development project team is responsible for developing their own budget, since it is the individual members of the team who know best about the costs of their project (project driven budgeting). The project development board adjusts the project budget for the overall development portfolio. The development activities are adjusted to the financial frame set by the available budget. The resource allocation by the board is a revolving activity. It must be decided several times per year for each project whether to continue a project and with what intensity. For each development project a Drug Development Plan is set up, describing and defining all activities needed to reach the next decision point. The sum of the costs of anticipated resources, support activities, and indirect costs is the estimated total costs of the project for the given budget period. This sum is calculated under the assumption that all milestones will be successfully reached, and therefore exceeds the overall development budget. But since attrition is still very high in development, most projects will be eliminated at one of the many decision points during the budget period.

The probability of passing a given decision point can be estimated from past experience and is dependent on the project phase. 'Factoring' is the application of the probability percentage to the resources and costs for the time after the decision point. The full budget costs before the decision points and the factored costs after the decision point will provide the budget costs for the project in the given project period. The sum of all factored project costs will provide the necessary budget and must be compared to the budget framework. Exceeding the budget framework will result in revision of the portfolio and possibly in the termination of entire development projects.

The high attrition rate demands that R&D resources are well spent and unsuccessful projects terminated quickly. A predefined and elaborate R&D process has been developed, and every deviation from the expected results during the testing needs to be detected and investigated. If a drug candidate fails during the development phase it is entirely withdrawn from further testing. Unlike in the automobile industry, drugs are not modular products where a faulty stick shift can be replaced without throwing the entire car design away. In pharmaceutical R&D, drug design cannot be changed. This necessitates high up-front investment for each drug candidate.

## Managing Outsourcing Activities at Solvias

Outsourcing is expected to improve speed as well as capacity and capability shortages during drug discovery and development. Major concerns of pharmaceutical companies, which in turn should be addressed by the pharmaceutical service provider, include complexity and efficiency, intellectual property and royalties, exclusivity and costs. Hence, the success factors for service providers imply a clear definition of efficient and highly standardized processes and contracts. Furthermore, a cooperation agreement has to be signed which avoids royalties and leaves all intellectual property at the pharmaceutical company. Clear non-disclosure agreements and non-competitive agreements in the field of chemical substances have to be established; as well as a comprehensive and full cost transparency.

The service provider Solvias was created through the spin-off of a scientific competence center of Novartis in October 1999 and is a totally independent company owned by the Solvias management. Today, the company employs around 250 highly qualified employees. Solvias offers services to the pharmaceutical industry mainly in the areas of research and development, production and quality control. The company's services include a variety of chemical, physical and biological services – from synthesis to analytics. Solvias provides its services to companies from the pharmaceutical, agricultural, chemical and food industries as well as government authorities and institutes. Clients include Beiersdorf, Boehringer Ingelheim, Roche, Shell and Wella among others.

Solvias differentiates between three cooperation models between the pharmaceutical company and the pharmaceutical service provider, depending on the amount and price of services provided (Fig. 40). With the preferred partnership model, the customer (pharmaceutical company) enters into preferential agreements with a handful of selected, strategic suppliers acting almost as 'facility managers'. However, this model might clash with the pharmaceutical company's desire to keep a certain level of freedom, as well as to maintain a healthy bargaining power vis-à-vis vendors. The second model, the 'a la carte'- drawing from a list of pre-selected vendors, is usually applied if no single supplier is able to provide the breadth of capabilities required by the pharmaceutical company to serve its full spectrum of needs. Overdependence on a single vendor should be avoided so as to spread risks and maintain a healthy leverage. The best vendor for each area of activity should be retained by the customer. The antagonist-model provides the pharmaceutical company with the advantage that the vendors (service providers) are systematically put into competition and, hence, the best price for the offered service can be secured.

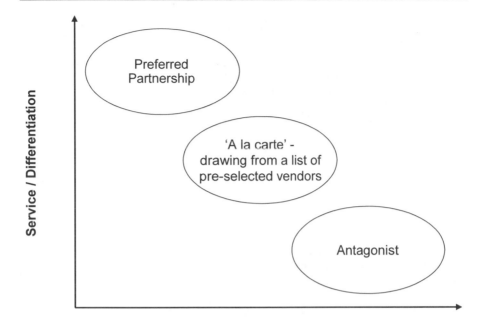

**Fig. 40.** Main models of customer-vendor interaction in outsourcing pharmaceutical R&D (Example: Solvias).

No matter which model and what degree of outsourcing is being applied, the service provider should always be fully integrated into the processes and structures of the pharmaceutical company. Areas with a high potential of standardization are of interest for outsourcing, such as processes, interfaces, contracts, and incentives. If, however, there is a high level of complexity in the processes between service provider and pharmaceutical company, or if there are interfaces that are difficult to define, the tendency towards outsourcing declines. The establishment of an effective and efficient interface between the pharmaceutical company and the service provider is therefore key to success for any outsourcing agreement.

For synthesis services, it has been shown that the chemical structure (as written on paper) represents the most appropriate interface. The service provider takes over the synthetic chemistry of the development process and delivers the chemical substances back to the pharmaceutical company (see Fig. 41).

However, a clear distinction must be drawn between development services and production services. Primary development services include proc-

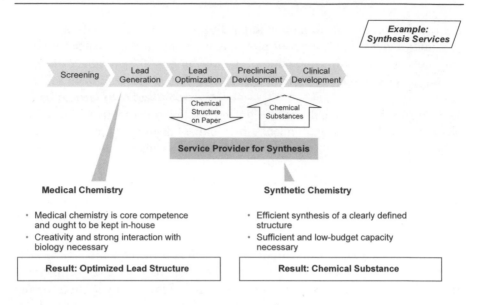

**Fig. 41.** Interface between pharmaceutical company and pharmaceutical service provider: Example of synthesis services provided by Solvias.

ess research & development, development of second generation processes as well as the supply of pre-clinical trial quantities. Primary production related services are dealing with the full scale supply of intermediates and active pharmaceutical ingredients (APIs) at various stages of the product lifecycle (Fig. 42).

In the future, it is expected that external service providers may even temporarily be integrated into internal R&D teams and, hence, will be able to provide more flexibly and timely support for R&D projects. The responsibility for the effective and efficient coordination of all internal and external resources as well as the know-how and expertise transfer will be represented by an internal project management, which is regarded as a core competence of the pharmaceutical company. There are different consequences of this paradigm shift. Barriers between the individual organization units and the various companies will disappear. In the long run, pharmaceutical and biotechnology companies will have a greater possibility to buy standardized and established external services or new and innovative methods around chemical synthesis along the entire value chain in pharmaceutical R&D. Therefore, pharmaceutical R&D will become leaner and will be able to avoid building and maintaining research infrastructure that is used in parallel.

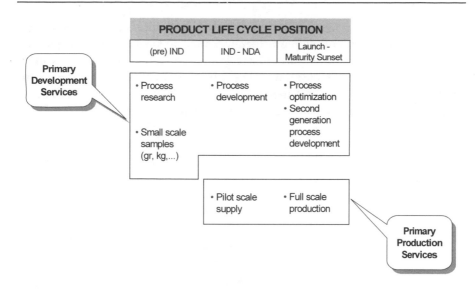

**Fig. 42.** Distinction between development and production services at Solvias.

## Managing Intellectual Property Rights at Bayer

Besides making inventions available to the public, intellectual property rights, patents and trademarks fulfill another important role: It assigns ownership to an individual and thus establishes the legal basis for commercial benefits to the inventor; through enforcement of intellectual property rights, the law protects innovators against imitation and replication of their innovations and knowledge. This protection is crucial in the pharmaceutical industry as otherwise nobody would invest in expensive and long-term drug development. Why should a firm invest US$ 800 million into a new drug if generics manufacturers imitate it a few months later? Granted, the profits made from successful drugs are impressive; they have led to a demonization of pharma giants akin to an evil empire and garnered substantial popular reaction. However, only few drug candidates ever become successful at all, and it is in the nature of the drug development process and the inalienable principle of drug safety that product development takes this much time and money to complete.

In the pharmaceutical industry, drugs and medicines can easily be copied or imitated because it is not difficult to analyze a pharmaceutical product and determine its respective substances. Due to the significant R&D

spending in the pharmaceutical industry and the high risks associated with new drug development, patent protection and the subsequent management of intellectual property is particularly important in this industry. As mentioned earlier, studies have shown that patents are the most effective means of appropriation and found that 65 percent of pharmaceutical inventions would not have been introduced without patent protection, compared to a cross-industry average of 8 percent (Reuters 2002). Unless intellectual property is protected with the outmost care, pharmaceutical innovation would not take place as we know it, and overall quality of life (and death) would be significantly reduced. The negative impact for the society would be dramatic.

The 40 leading pharmaceutical firms worldwide have been granted on average 5.8 patents per thousand employees. In 2001, the U.S. accounted for approximately 45 percent of all pharmaceutical patents that were issued. Japan and Germany both contributed around 10 percent of patents, followed by the UK with 7 percent and France with 5 percent. Looking at company trends, U.S. companies continue to dominate patent approvals in the US. The proportion of U.S. pharmaceutical patents issued to U.S. and Japanese companies has increased over the last 20 years, while the proportion issued to European companies has declined: Between 1980 and 1984, U.S. companies were issued around 50 percent of patents, Japanese companies 13 percent and EU companies 29 percent. However, between 1990 and 1994, the proportion of patents issued to U.S. and Japanese companies increased to 55 percent and 15 percent respectively, while the proportion issued to EU companies fell to 24 percent (Reuters 2002).

Leading therapy areas for patent approval worldwide were infectious disease (15%), oncology (14%), cardiovascular disease (10%), neurology (10%), and immune disorders (8%). The distribution of patents across therapy areas largely reflects the balance of the pipeline, and is closely matched to relative unmet need and market opportunity (Reuters 2002).

International patent legislation typically encompasses four statutory classes of patentable inventions that are relevant to the pharmaceutical industry (see Reuters 2003b):

- Process patents;
- Product patents;
- Composition patents;
- Use patents.

Process claims refer to the method used to produce a pharmaceutical product rather than to the chemical itself. As it may be possible to develop the same chemical through several different methods, it is often difficult to protect pharmaceutical products solely with process patents or to prove infringement of process patents. Product patents refer to tangible products. Generally, these are commercially viable entities that are ready to be launched or already on the market.

In the pharmaceutical industry, patents are usually applied to medical devices, such as drug delivery mechanisms, since few manufacturers would want to wait until they perform clinical trials on a compound to apply for patent protection. Depending on the territory of filing, new substances or new processes receive patent protection for a period of 20 years (e.g., by the FDA in the U.S.). However, considering that the average time for drug development in the pharmaceutical industry can reach up to 13 years, the major problem regarding patent protection becomes obvious: the timing of the patent. If a company files for a patent too early, the period when it can market and sell the drug exclusively will automatically be reduced. This is particularly important in light of the fact that pharmaceutical companies only have a relatively short time to market their products and generate a return on their high initial investments. On the other hand, if a company files too late for a patent, it risks losing the invention to competitors. In practice, this means that the effective period of patent protection is rarely more than 8 years in the pharmaceutical industry (see also page 57). Sophisticated methods and techniques to deal with intellectual property are therefore a necessity.

The following case example of Bayer illustrates how a pharmaceutical company can utilize and maximize the value generated by its intellectual property by taking a proactive approach to commercialize its intellectual property generated. In this context, Bayer looks at intellectual property as a product of its own. Every intellectual property thus needs its own marketing plan. The intellectual property products are typically spin-offs, 'whitespace' developments or technologies (i.e., devices or methods) that are no longer being used by Bayer's business units. When selling the products, Bayer strictly follows the rule, 'don't try to sell any leftovers'.

Bayer developed a four-stage process to decide if certain know-how or a certain technology can be utilized externally (Fig. 43). First, Bayer asks if the respective know-how/technology is a surplus product. If yes, the second stage contemplates if the know-how is strategically valuable for any core activity of Bayer's business units. If it is not, the third stage analyzes if the respective technology could be easily brought to a potentially attractive market. If this stage is answered with a yes, the final stage observes if the know-how is not strategically valuable for any other business unit at Bayer. If the intellectual property passes all four stages, it can be marketed outside of Bayer, otherwise it is retained in-house.

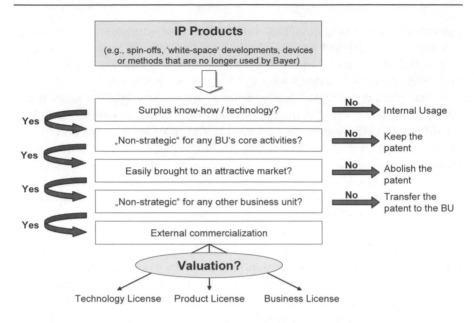

**Fig. 43.** Process to commercialize intellectual property at Bayer.

Regarding the valuation of the intellectual property, Bayer differentiates between business licenses, product licenses, and technology licenses. The value of business and product licenses, which deal with entire businesses and/or products, can easily be determined by using the scenario technique. The value of technology licenses, however, is much more complicated to estimate and done by looking at the technology maturity and the commercial risk. The combination of both allows for a fairly good estimate. Finally, the marketing plan includes the intellectual property utilization strategy, which could include cross-licensing agreements, royalty payments, cash payments, or equity offerings.

In general, patent protection becomes particularly important in the area of biotechnology. Several ethical questions arise that are not yet covered by existing patent laws and/or acts, including the ownership of genes and whether genes can be patented at all. For example, the Swiss Ethics Committee on Non-Human Gene Technology recently came to the conclusion that intellectual achievements in the area of biotechnology are allowed to be protected. This is justified by the overall purpose of the patent act to support research in the best interest of the public. While it is possible today to receive patents for biotechnological inventions, such as a gene, a genetically changed plant, a biotechnological process or a microorganism, some inventions are excluded from patenting: processes regarding cloning of human beings, processes regarding changes of the genetic identity of human beings, as well as the usage of human embryos for industrial or commercial purposes.

## Managing Out-licensing at Novartis

About a decade ago (in 1998), researchers at Novartis came up with a new substance (Aliskiren) that was about to enter development stages, but Novartis' R&D management decided to stop the project. However, a team of Novartis' employees around Dr. Alice Huxley – then Global Project Manager at Novartis – strongly believed in the substance and was interested in pursuing this opportunity further. Subsequently, they left Novartis, started to set up their own company called Speedel and in-licensed the substance from Novartis. Today, Speedel employs around 75 employees and became a publicly traded company at the Swiss Stock Exchange in 2005. While Novartis initially stopped Aliskiren's development, they looked at this out-licensing opportunity with Speedel as an opportunity to continue the substance's development with a low risk exposure as the licensing agreement would transfer the development risks to Speedel.

All out-licensing efforts at Novartis are organizationally embedded in the firm's Business Development & Licensing department (BD&L). This department deploys 80 employees whereas 3 persons are responsible for out-licensing. Compared to in-licensing, the importance of out-licensing seems to be fairly low. However, Novartis considers out-licensing as an important issue in order to add economic value to idle substances. Novartis usually decides to license out a substance due to one of the following rationales:

- The substance is not strategically relevant any more;
- The substance does not fulfill the required performance potential;
- New substances arise which cannot be pursued any further within the scope of Novartis and without making significant upfront investments in infrastructure and know-how.

The primary objective of out-licensing is to at least recoup the costs which have been incurred for the respective substances so far. In addition, Novartis expects to achieve additional benefits and royalty revenues in case the collaboration partner successfully introduces the new substance on the market. For this reason, Novartis always includes revenue participation clauses or re-licensing options in any out-licensing contracts. Regarding the decision which substance should be out-licensed, Novartis conducts market dynamics analyses including the observation of competitors' activities. Particularly the substances that have already dissipated significant resources are of interest for out-licensing because this could be the only way to at least generate some kind of payback. Therefore, it is not unusual within Novartis that the project teams themselves suggest out-licensing a stopped substance in order to see at least some kind of success for the huge amount of work they have already put into the substance's research and development.

Novartis sees particular benefits in licensing out to smaller companies. These firms are usually very interested in Novartis' substances because their reputation increases significantly if they announce a licensing deal with Novartis. This in turn makes it much easier for the partner firms to secure funding from other investors.

## Out-licensing as a 10-step process

Novartis uses a standardized out-licensing process (see Fig. 44). The out-licensing process comprises 10 steps. First, a cross-functionally staffed committee decides which substance might potentially be out-licensed. The head of the Business Development & Licensing department is always participating during this step. While the decision committee based in Basel decides about out-licensing of all global development projects, there are also local teams that might evaluate and decide about licensing out a substance targeting a relatively small local market. After the decision committee has come to the conclusion to license out a substance, a team around the Head of Drug Delivery Licensing & Out-licensing comes into play. This team creates a brief product profile of the substance that should be out-licensed (only around 2-3 pages) aggregating the most important non-confidential product information. This product profile contains information about the already conducted development activities as well as data about projected potentials.

During a subsequent step, Novartis identifies possible licensing partners. This search is done by screening through all sorts of information (publicly available as well as internally available) about other bio-pharmaceutical companies and their respective R&D activities. The possible licensing partners are evaluated and assessed according to their competencies and capabilities to pursue the further development of the drug candidate. This evaluation and assessment mainly – but not exclusively – includes financial aspects.

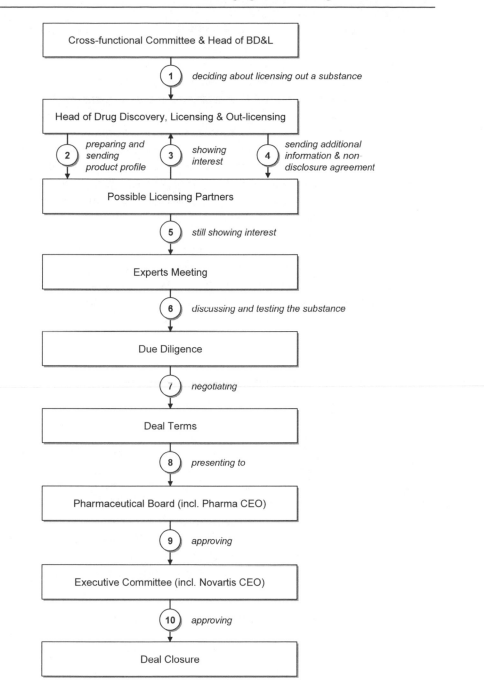

Source: Reepmeyer (2005)

**Fig. 44.** Out-licensing process at Novartis.

After the identification of some possible licensing partners, the potential licensees receive the previously prepared product profile with a non-binding inquiry about the out-licensing opportunity. While some substances usually attract statements of interest within a relatively short period of time, other substances might be available for out-licensing for several years. In case no partner can be found, these substances are withdrawn and the projects are terminated. If a possible licensing partner shows a first interest in a certain substance, Novartis signs a non-disclosure agreement with this company. It can be the case that Novartis signs different non-disclosure agreements with multiple partners. After having signed these agreements, Novartis sends a confidential and detailed documentation about the substance to each partner. If a partner is still interested after having read the additional documentation, the first personal interaction between Novartis and the potential partner takes place. Experts of both firms meet and discuss the substance including the chances and risks associated with the drug's development. In some cases, Novartis might also send small probations of the substance (a few milligrams or grams) to the partner. This allows the partner to practically proof the substance with in-vitro or in-vivo trials.[*]

If there are still several partners interested in the substance after this stage of the out-licensing process, the more powerful partners are invited for due diligence negotiations. The typical due diligence takes place at Novartis and lasts about 1 or 2 days. It can be the case that Novartis negotiates with two partners simultaneously at the same time. After this step, Novartis and the potential partner discuss the key terms of the licensing agreement. If the partners agree on the terms, the Head of Drug Delivery Licensing & Out-licensing gives an internal presentation of the entire process to the pharmaceutical board including the CEO of the pharmaceutical division. If the pharmaceutical board approves the deal, the pharma CEO presents the deal towards the Novartis Executive Committee under the supervision of Novartis' CEO, Daniel Vasella. This committee ultimately approves the deal. However, the Executive Committee reserved the right to retrospectively stop or terminate any out-licensing project.

## Characteristics of an out-licensing contract

The actual out-licensing contract is prepared by the Head of Drug Delivery Licensing & Out-licensing, a corporate lawyer, a person from the patent

---

[*] While in-vitro trials analyze a substance in test-tubes, in-vivo experiments use living organisms.

department as well as a key scientist. A contract usually covers 50-60 pages. Novartis generally differentiates between two types of contracts. Firstly, the option-licensing-agreement, which gives the partner an option for a product license. In this scenario, the partner can proof if it can successfully pursue the further development of the underlying substance and decides at a later point in time about the definite purchase of the license. Secondly, the licensing-agreement, which includes a traditional licensing contract right from the beginning. The contract typically covers upfront payments, milestone payments and royalty revenues. The highest milestone payments occur if the substance finally reaches the market.

The link between Novartis and the partner throughout the collaboration is formed by a so-called Key Contact Person. For some larger deals, Novartis creates a Steering Committee comprised of BD&L employees which follows the same purpose as the Key Contact Person in observing the progress of the substance at the licensing partner. The Key Contact Person or Steering Committee respectively observe in semi-annual and annual analyses if the contractual agreements are still met. Typically, Novartis is contractually allowed to withdraw from a licensing deal if certain targets and milestones are not met.

Risk considerations play a crucial role for out-licensing at Novartis. While out-licensing represents the risk that an initially internally developed substance might generate significant revenues for an external partner at some point in time, Novartis is exposed to the risk of not being able to participate in this upside potential. In order to manage this risk of a potentially wrong projection of the drug's potential, Novartis usually retains a call-back option in any out-licensing contract. The point in time when Novartis would like to use its call-back option is usually stated in the contract. The call-back option differs across different substances depending on product-specific development risks, the substance's market potential, or the performance potential of the licensee. The call-back will usually occur if the risks for further development of the substance are low enough in order to justify the call-back and further internal development. This point in time is usually somewhere between Phase II and the end of the development process. In case the point in time for the call-back is not part of the contract, Novartis reserves the right to start re-licensing negotiations depending on the individual situation of the substance's development.

The entire out-licensing process from the initial negotiations of the key terms through the deal closure usually lasts between 6 to 9 months. Searching and screening for the partner is not included in this time period. Novartis' stakeholders are also included throughout the entire out-licensing process. The units which are affected by the out-licensing deal can give their comments and critics at any time.

## Structure of the out-licensing collaboration with Speedel

In 1999 (after Speedel had been set up and started operations), Novartis out-licensed to Speedel the substance Aliskiren (SPP100), which targets cardiovascular indications. Aliskiren is an oral renin inhibitor that has demonstrated exciting potential for the treatment of hypertension. Today's market for antihypertensives represents approximately US$ 40 billion or about 40 percent of the entire cardiovascular market. It is expected to reach US$ 50 billion by 2009 (Speedel 2004). Hypertension affects more than 135 million people in the developed world. It is a major cause of strokes, chronic renal disease, congestive heart failure and myocardial infarction. Renin inhibitors, such as Aliskiren, work by regulating the kidney's production of renin. Renin, an enzyme, is associated with the release of a second substance that narrows blood vessels, making it harder for blood to flow through the arteries and raising blood pressure. Aliskiren suppresses the release of renin – and thus keeps blood pressure in a normal range.

After Novartis had out-licensed the substance Aliskiren, Speedel started performing the respective development activities for Aliskiren's clinical phases I and II. In total, Speedel conducted 18 clinical studies comprising about 500 patients and healthy volunteers. In addition to pilot studies in chronic renal failure and heart failure, Speedel ran a 4-week, 220-patient Phase II study that compared the compound to Merck & Co.'s Losartan (Cozaar); the two substances showed similar blood-pressure lowering effects. Crucially, Speedel was the first company to establish clinical proof of concept in Phase II and to have developed and patented a commercially viable manufacturing process for a renin inhibitor, an area of industry research for over 20 years.

Throughout the duration of the collaboration, Novartis retained a call-back option to license the substance back at any stage of development. As Novartis was pleased by the positive development results, the company exercised the call-back option for the compound in September 2002 (see Fig. 45). In November 2003, Novartis announced that its was moving Aliskiren into clinical phase III trials, which were initiated in March 2004. This left Speedel with significant milestone payments due to the successful development in Phase I and II. The amount of the milestone payments, which Speedel received from Novartis in July 2004 was not disclosed. However, they included a cash element and an equity participation. In January 2005, Novartis announced positive data from the Phase III study of Aliskiren as a monotherapy for the treatment of hypertension, and positive Phase II data from a combination study of Aliskiren with Diovan, another anti-hypertensive compound which is Novartis' leading drug. Novartis filed for regulatory approval in 2006, and received market approval for

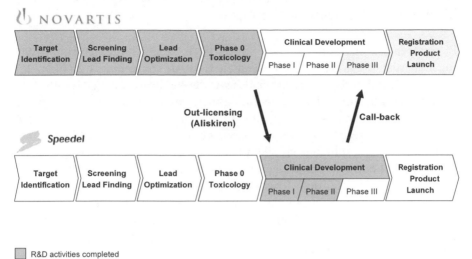

Source: Reepmeyer (2005)

**Fig. 45.** Out-licensing collaboration between Novartis and Speedel.

Aliskiren in the U.S. in 2007. The drug's market launch will ultimately benefit both companies Novartis and Speedel.

In summary, Novartis' out-licensing approach enabled the company to increase its 'shots on goal' without simply enlarging their already significant in-house R&D budgets. The success of the collaboration with Speedel demonstrates how the continuing disintegration of the pharmaceutical value chain creates new partnership models which allow the pharmaceutical company to leverage not only its own core competencies, but also the strengths of its partners. One of the most notable issues during this collaboration was the fact that Speedel had been a relatively young company which did not have a track record regarding the successful execution of drug development projects at the time of the deal closure. Thus, Novartis sold the compound Aliskiren to a company for further development although it was not sure whether the partner firm would be able to successfully execute the compound's development. The fact that Speedel's management team had previously been with Novartis was one of the main reasons why Novartis trusted Speedel to be able to turn the substance into a success.

## Managing Uncertainty at Roche

Pharmaceutical research is moving away from the classical concept of having expertise in a certain disease area towards increasingly applied research. New expert knowledge and basic research are being brought into research organizations by collaborations and interactions with universities and small biotechnology companies. In addition, more emphasis is placed on providing novel tools for research such as high-throughput screening, genomics and combinatorial chemistry. Especially at the front-end of R&D, virtual partnerships are entered with biotechnology companies.

The goals of virtual R&D partnership are a higher flexibility to choose the best R&D service providers, spreading of risk and costs, and economies of scale and scope. Companies try to reduce their fixed costs through transfer of less intensively utilized services to learning partner companies. This has two major advantages, namely

1. A reduction of internal complexity due to concentration, and
2. A reduction of external interfaces, since the task is now shared with the partner companies.

Roche outsourced much of the R&D process to specialized partners and suppliers, or has set-up focused R&D service providers. Examples of spin-offs of corporate R&D at Roche include Actelion and BioXell. In 1996, Roche established Protodigm, a 'virtual drug development company' (Hofmann 1997) in London. In one instance, Protodigm learned of a certain molecule, a prospective new medical substance, discovered in a university laboratory and then facilitated further research by guiding the R&D process. It contacted specialized companies to test the substance, coordinated the first clinical trials, and contracted out production, second-stage clinical development, manufacturability tests, drug registration, marketing, and even sales.

The ten Protodigm employees simultaneously oversaw three future drugs in various stages of pharmaceutical development. Since Protodigm chose the most qualified subcontractor for each stage of R&D, Roche expected a reduction in R&D costs and development time. The objective was to cut R&D costs by 40 percent without jeopardizing the already tight development schedule. Protodigm became Fulcrum-Pharma in 2001, expanding to offices in Japan and the US. Roche was not the only pharmaceutical company experimenting with virtual R&D: Merck was said to have saved US$ 170 million with this type of outsourcing in 1996 alone.

Behind this tendency is a fundamental change in the pharmaceutical industry: Basic research and coordination of clinical trials is increasingly being sourced out to universities or specialized companies. The industry is in the midst of changing from vertically integrated competition towards horizontal-type competition like the PC industry. Sophisticated physical models replace trial and error experiments through simulation on powerful computers.

Virtual R&D is facilitated by shared information and communication technologies networks (to expedite information and data exchange), the standardization of interfaces, and the high quality of the work carried out by the different members of the network. Information in the form of knowledge about technologies and products, customer feedback, product tests, research results, and markets, all must be collected, analyzed, and transferred. This information must be available in a codified, quantified or explicit form (see Nonaka and Takeuchi 1995). Implicit or tacit knowledge, which is difficult to articulate because of its ambiguity and context-relatedness, is much harder to transfer. Systemic innovation with its late 'freezing points' requires the interaction and integration of different knowledge sources and presents a great challenge for multi-site R&D.

Therefore, R&D can be 'virtualized' only if innovation is autonomous, if there are few interdependencies between parallel work tasks. Systemic innovations (i.e., R&D that involves the realization and adaptation of complementing technologies with complex interfaces) are more effectively done in large companies with central R&D. If an autonomous innovation is carried out by a centralized organization, the company is usually outrun by small firms or large decentralized companies.

Virtual R&D has thus grown in importance, in particular in industries characterized by rapidly advancing technologies, relative scarcity of technical talent, and the presence of more and more codified information in the innovation process: mostly in the electronics, information technology, software, pharmaceutical and chemical industries.

## Managing Global R&D at Major Swiss Pharma Companies

### Switzerland as R&D location

Switzerland is an attractive location for pharmaceutical research and development. The three Interpharma* companies Novartis, Roche and Serono invest around 40 percent of their global R&D spending in Switzerland. The geographic concentration of the pharmaceutical industry in the north-

---

* Interpharma is Switzerland's association for research-based pharmaceutical companies.

west of Switzerland, its proximity to a large number of other small and mid-size companies in the broadly defined healthcare segment, and its proximity to very good research centers within universities are central reasons why Switzerland is an excellent pharmaceutical R&D location (creation of innovation clusters).

The increase in the number of small and mid-size biotechnology companies in Switzerland has become another significantly important factor. In general, the nature of biotechnology firms is to focus on research because they are still developing their initial products. Marketing and sales forces grow only when a viable product nears government approval. Hence, the approximately 140 biotechnology firms in Switzerland represent a great pool of resources for R&D activities and highlight Switzerland's worldwide importance as an R&D location.

Besides close interactions between biotechnology and pharmaceutical companies, Swiss science is among the most recognized regarding pharmaceutical fundamental research. The Swiss Scientific Council (Schweizer Wissenschaftsrat) compared fundamental research in Switzerland to other OECD countries. A citation-index providing information on how often scientific papers are quoted by other scientists (total number of quotes divided by number of publications) was calculated. The source of this research was a database of the Institute for Scientific Information (ISI, Philadelphia) from 1994 to 1998. About 5,000 scientific journals ranging from medicine and mathematics, 1,500 scientific journals about social sciences and another 1,100 journals from humanities and arts were included in the database. The results revealed that Switzerland owned a leading role in seven different disciplines related to fundamental biopharmaceutical research, including molecular biology / genetics, immunology, pharmacology, chemistry, physics, botany / zoology, ecology and environmental studies.

## Pharmaceutical R&D spending in Switzerland

According to the Swiss Federal Office for Statistics (Bundesamt für Statistik), total expenditures for research and development activities within Switzerland were US$ 7,605 million in 2004. The private sector accounted for about 70 percent, the public authorities for 23 percent and other institutions for 7 percent. Hence, the bulk of research and development expenditures is contributed by private organizations.

According to Economiesuisse (2006), private R&D expenditures can be differentiated into intramuros expenditures, extramuros expenditures, and R&D expenditures of foreign subsidiaries of Swiss firms. While intramuros expenditures cover R&D expenses spent by a firm for its own R&D labs inside Switzerland, extramuros expenditures cover R&D jobs out-sourced to third parties either within Switzerland or abroad.

The pharmaceutical-chemical industry accounted for US$ 3,347 million or 44 percent of intramuros R&D expenditures as well as for US$ 2,467 million or 78 percent of extramuros R&D expenditures in 2004 (see Fig. 46). Out of the US$ 2,467 million extramuros R&D expenditures, the pharmaceutical-chemical industry spent about 58 percent on research projects abroad compared with just 42 percent in 1996. Out of the US$ 7,561 million in R&D spending by Swiss companies abroad, the pharmaceutical-chemical industry covers 77 percent or US$ 5,796 million (Economie-suisse 2006). This further stresses the significant shift in R&D spending by Swiss pharmaceutical-chemical companies towards foreign subsidiaries.

Out of the US$ 3,347 million of total intramuros R&D spending in the pharmaceutical-chemical industry, about US$ 1,600 million was spent on

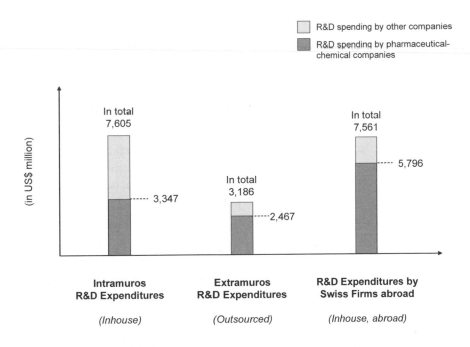

Source: Economiesuisse (2006)

**Fig. 46.** R&D spending by Swiss pharmaceutical-chemical companies in 2004.

experimental development, US$ 1,000 million on applied research and another US$ 775 million on fundamental research.

R&D spending in biotechnology increased to around US$ 654 million in 2004. Pharmaceutical-chemical companies as well as research laboratories accounted for 88 percent of this amount, which again highlights the close interactions between pharmaceutical firms and biotechnology firms.

Of 33,084 people (in person-years) working in R&D in Switzerland, the pharmaceutical-chemical industry employs 6,000 people or 18 percent of the total R&D workforce in Switzerland in 2004, this is compared to 11,360 or 30.4 percent in 1996. Hence, the pharmaceutical-chemical industry has been scaling down its R&D staff in Switzerland over the past years. About 47 percent of R&D employees in Switzerland have a college/university degree. Of 6,000 people working in R&D in the pharmaceutical-chemical industry in Switzerland, about 54 percent are foreigners compared to an average of 32 percent of foreigners for all industries. Two-thirds (61%) of foreign employees working in the pharmaceutical-chemical industry in Switzerland hold a college/university degree.

In 2001, the three Swiss Interpharma companies – Novartis, Roche and Serono – sold drugs worth CHF 507 million in Switzerland, just 1.2 percent of their global sales. Nonetheless, Novartis, Roche and Serono spent almost CHF 3.1 billion on pharmaceutical research and development in Switzerland in the same year. This represents around 43.3 percent of their global outlay on pharmaceutical R&D and is roughly equivalent to their pharmaceutical R&D spending in the US. However, more recently the U.S. and the Far East seem to have become increasingly important to the Interpharma companies, as recent R&D investments in Boston (Novartis) and Shanghai (Roche) illustrate. The high outlay for research and development in Switzerland is only possible because of the high export volume in the pharmaceutical sector. In 2001, Novartis, Roche and Serono together exported around CHF 25 billion in pharmaceutical products, 90 percent of Switzerland's total pharmaceutical exports.

## International R&D management at Novartis

Novartis deploys several research centers worldwide which can be classified to one of the following four research institute groups:

- Novartis Institutes for BioMedical Research (NIBR);
- The Genomics Institute of the Novartis Research Foundation (GNF);
- Novartis Institute for Tropical Diseases (NITD);
- Friedrich Miescher Institute (FMI).

Pharmaceutical research is primarily conducted through the Novartis Institutes for BioMedical Research, led by Mark Fishman, professor at the Harvard Medical School. The Novartis Institutes for BioMedical Research are headquartered in Cambridge, Massachusetts, and have several locations around the world. The Cambridge facility currently houses over 1,300 scientists and technology experts. The Cambridge headquarters will continue to grow, with a US$ 4 billion investment planned over a period of 10 years. Aligned with the corporate world headquarters, Novartis Institutes in Basel are an integral part of the BioValley, Europe's biotechnology hub. This research facility houses approximately 1 500 temporary and permanent research associates. The other main Novartis Research Institutes are located in East Hanover (US), Horsham (UK, focus on respiratory disease), Vienna (AU, focus on dermatology), Tsukuba (JP, focus on arthritis), and London (UK, focus on pain). NIBR is planning a new location in Shanghai focused on diseases prevalent in China and Asia. The choice to locate a new R&D site in Cambridge – as opposed to expanding the existing research centers in East Hanover (New Jersey) or Basel (Switzerland) – was made with consideration to the vast and so far untapped concentration of biomedical scientists, hospitals, research institutes, and corporate R&D centers in Cambridge. In comparison to California, for instance, the Boston-Cambridge area also has a higher concentration of biotech firms in a five- to ten-mile radius. With the joint appointment of Mark Fishman as the new head of biomedical research at Novartis worldwide, a significant power shift has occurred from Basel to Cambridge.

The Genomics Institute of the Novartis Research Foundation (GNF) in La Jolla, California, is known for developing advanced technologies, ranging from cellular genomics and proteomics to combinatorial chemistry and structural biology. The mission of GNF is to exploit these technologies to identify new biological processes and understand the underlying mechanisms involved in human disease. These discoveries are being translated into human therapeutics by a preclinical drug discovery effort. GNF was founded in 1999 and currently houses over 400 employees. In addition to its internal resources, the Institute is located near the Scripps Research Institute and other international researchers in southern California.

The Novartis Institute for Tropical Diseases (NITD) in Singapore aims to discover novel treatments and prevention methods for major tropical diseases. Novartis intends to make treatments readily available without profit in those developing countries where these diseases are endemic. The scope of Novartis' activities range from target discovery through to screen development and compound optimization. The Institute – set up as a center of excellence – will offer teaching and training opportunities for postdoctoral fellows and graduate students. Novartis' long-term objective is to help reduce the overall affliction of tropical diseases and ultimately, improve the prosperity of developing countries. Dengue Fever and tuberculosis were collectively selected as the diseases on which to focus, with the possibility to expand to other disease areas in later years.

The Friedrich Miescher Institute (founded in 1970) is devoted to fundamental biomedical research. Novartis employs new technologies to explore basic molecular mechanisms of cells and organisms in health and disease. Research focuses on the fields of epigenetics, growth control and neurobiology. The institute is an internationally recognized research center that has initiated key developments in molecular biology over the years. It also provides young scientists an opportunity to participate in scientific research at the post-graduate and postdoctoral levels.

According to Savioz (2002), all R&D activities at Novartis are fully decentralized to sectors. R&D at Novartis Pharma is organized by a matrix of three dimensions: therapeutic areas, core technologies and senior experts. Those responsible for general coordination of these three R&D dimension meet monthly as the Research Management Board, consisting of heads of therapeutic areas, heads of core technologies, senior experts and the head of research. Project decisions, in particular rough resource allocation, are the main focus of this board meeting. However, therapeutic areas and core technologies are quite independent of strategic planning and 'detailed' resource allocation. Thus, this is a bottom-up process that is 'controlled' by an upper level. R&D activities within these three dimensions are dispersed among several global research centers, mainly in Europe and the USA. Besides internal R&D activities, Novartis Pharma maintains a cooperation network. At the group level a central 'Group Technology' coordinates the sector's technology strategies, detects synergy potentials, and is responsible for knowledge management and generation of new businesses. This group is supported by two scientific advisory boards, the Research Advisory Board for product technology purposes and the Technology Advisory Board for process technology purposes, which include, among other members, the key heads of R&D and production. In summary, the most important characteristics of R&D and technology management are:

- Decentralized sectors and therefore very international R&D;
- Projects that are financed by sectors, some budgets for new technologies at the group level;
- Participative planning in sectors, coordination of synergies at the group level;
- Science-based and technology-driven business;
- Market-driven innovation culture as well as bottom-up-driven decision-making culture.

Development and marketing are integrated into discovery at start of product continuum and are an important part of research portfolio reviews. Novartis relies on multidisciplinary groups of researchers to solve target structures and focus on designing drugs rationally. This reduces the number of compounds that are tested to find a successful one. Groups are divided into four general sections – structured bioinformatics, molecular modeling, protein expression and purification, and those that perform structural biology work – these groups work in collaboration rather than sitting in specialized groups.

## Managing a Niche-Market Strategy at Intarcia

As already pointed out in earlier chapters, some of today's most successful biopharmaceutical companies pursue very focused niche-market strategies centering around specialized and highly selective compounds and markets. These firms apply different approaches to access these markets either with specialized sales forces or by focusing on unique product offerings. Intarcia Therapeutics, a small biopharmaceutical company located in Emeryville, California, represents a good example how a company can successfully apply a niche-market strategy.

Intarcia was initially founded in 1995 under the name BioMedicines and started operations in 1997. In 2006, Intarcia had 35 full-time employees, 25 of whom are engaged in research and development activities or direct support thereof. Since the company's inception, Intarcia has principally been funded through the sale of more than $195 million of the company's stock. Investors in the firm include several venture capital firms.

Intarcia applies an innovative and targeted approach to the acquisition, development and commercialization of novel therapeutic products for the treatment of cancer and infectious diseases. The company uses its expertise in clinical medicine, pharmaceutical development and regulatory affairs to discover alternate clinical applications or development pathways for clinical stage products with validated mechanisms of action and existing clinical safety and activity data. Intarcia then frequently combines these products with other products or technologies to create new therapeutic products that address significant market needs. Intarcia's business strategy involves to:

- *Acquire products with significant market potential:* This includes the identification, evaluation and purchase of product candidates which can be developed into therapeutics with superior characteristics compared to existing therapies. Intarcia expects that there is usually less competition for product candidates for which alternate clinical applications could have been discovered or development pathways could not have been identified by their originators. This translates in both lower acquisition costs and future financial obligations. In addition, when the company acquires product candidates with validated mechanisms of action and significant existing safety and clinical data, the firm's early clinical development risk is reduced.

- *Advance programs through development:* Intarcia's management team has distinctive expertise in drug development covering biology and clinical medicine, clinical development and regulatory affairs, pharmacology, as well as formulation and drug delivery.
- *Maximize the commercial potential of product candidates:* After product approval, Intarcia intends to maximize the commercial opportunity for the product by either (i) building an own U.S. sales and marketing organization, (ii) establishing strategic collaborations to market products, or (iii) increasing market opportunity by expanding the indications for the firm's therapeutics.

Intarcia currently applies its business approach to create and advance the clinical programs around its most promising therapy Omega DUROS. Omega DUROS therapy is being developed to improve the treatment against the hepatitis C virus (HCV) by offering a more convenient and potentially safer and more effective treatment. Omega DUROS therapy is designed to deliver a continuous and consistent dose of omega interferon for three months via the implantable DUROS device, a drug delivery technology developed by ALZA Corporation, and licensed to Intarcia for use in certain broad fields. Another product incorporating the DUROS technology has already been approved by the FDA for the palliative treatment of prostate cancer. Intarcia is also leveraging the DUROS technology in evaluating other drug development opportunities. The most advanced of these is focused on the delivery of GLP-1 and GLP-1 analogs with the DUROS device for the treatment of type 2 diabetes.

Intarcia's management executes its business strategy of redirected and expanded development by forming partnerships with multiple partners. Intarcia signed different development and/or commercialization agreements with Schering AG, ALZA, Boehringer Ingelheim, and the G.D. Searle subsidiary of Pharmacia (now Pfizer). During its own development activities, Intarcia also relies on third party service providers to conduct the clinical trials for its product candidates.

One of the most important characteristics that differentiate Intarcia from larger pharmaceutical companies includes its high flexibility. Due to its small size and mission to redirect the indication of licensed compounds, the company is much better able to analyze and determine the maximum value potential of a compound. Intarcia can be more creative in finding delivery techniques in concert with other state-of-the-art technology platforms. According to Intarcia, the approach to 'think outside of the box' allows for more innovative ways to bring new drug candidates to market and, therefore, to commercialize research results. The commitment towards innovation at Intarcia is also expressed by the company's entrepreneurial culture which is highlighted by its highly venture-capital funded ownership structure as well as several equity incentive plans which entitle the employees to participate in the company's future success.

In addition, Intarcia believes that its ability to identify opportunities for its licensed drug candidates yield valuable insights that permit the firm to acquire, develop and commercialize its product candidates more rapidly and with significantly lower costs than traditional approaches to drug development. Moreover, the strategy of redirected development is often the most efficient and cost-effective means of advancing drugs rapidly into late stage development and commercialization. Therefore, Intarcia's strategy is not only innovative but also cost-effective. In addition, Intarcia is able to focus on much smaller markets which might be considered too small by many larger pharmaceutical firms.

## Managing Virtual Project Management Pools at Roche

Strategic pipeline management requires a strategic approach to managing researchers and research managers. Given the knowledge-intensive nature of pharmaceutical R&D, the management of human resources in pharmaceuticals has traditionally focused on developing specialists and reducing the (unwanted) flow of information beyond predetermined boundaries. More recently, however, the role of human resources has become to include, among others, personnel assessment and training, knowledge management, and strategic leadership development. All of these necessitate a more open-minded approach to managing people.

In the past decades, a paradigm shift has occurred in science. With the end of the cold war, fundamental industrial research ran out of government funds. At the same time, new entrepreneurial opportunities allowed young researchers to start commercializing their technologies themselves. Science became more open partly because of necessity (research labs reaching out for collaboration partners to sustain their innovation funnels) or because of opportunity (graduate students turned entrepreneurs seeking complementary technologies to start new businesses). While the pharmaceutical industry has followed or even developed this trend in outsourcing some of their basic research to biotechnology companies, they have often failed to rethink their internal R&D organizations to reflect the new times.

Small, multi-disciplinary teams have been at the core of the success of biotechnology start-ups or the introduction of new technologies. Large research and development departments are often good at administrating long-term research efforts, but incapable of flexible decision-making and absorption and dissemination of innovative ideas. Job rotation and training programs educate the individual researcher about other activities in the company, and allow him or her to make better and faster decisions: i.e., making decisions where the action is. For example, Bayer is known for their job rotation practice, where every researcher is only allowed to stay for a maximum of 5 years in the same position. Japanese pharmaceutical companies are also applying sophisticated job rotation programs. However, in many pharmaceutical companies, most of the researchers only have contact with the HR department once in a lifetime: at the moment they are hired.

Fostering creativity is another important aspect in managing human resources. Scientists spend only an estimated 11 percent of their time on research, and only 2 percent on new research. Chemists, microbiologists, medical doctors, and marketing experts should collaborate in new projects to learn from each other about the nature of their businesses. It is a long-established fact that interdisciplinary teams are better at innovation. Furthermore, it has been shown that creativity in pharmaceutical R&D is more likely in smaller research teams. The trend towards mega-mergers and ever larger companies forces pharmaceutical R&D management to bear in mind this parameter of creativeness.

The systematic promotion of human resource development strategies can be backed up by a specialized project management department as applied by Roche (Fig. 47). Roche's Pharma Division established a department called 'International Project Management' which coordinates a resource pool of about 50 project managers for all R&D projects worldwide. This department consumes about 30 percent of the pharmaceutical R&D expenditures and has high strategic importance to the innovative potential of this business.

Every project manager is assigned to this geographically decentralized department. The director of this 'virtual' resource pool assigns his/her people as managers to projects as part of a global program to ensure standards in quality and project procedures. Upon completion of the project, a project manager is returned to the resource pool. As there are more projects in the pipeline than managers available, they are immediately reassigned to a new project.

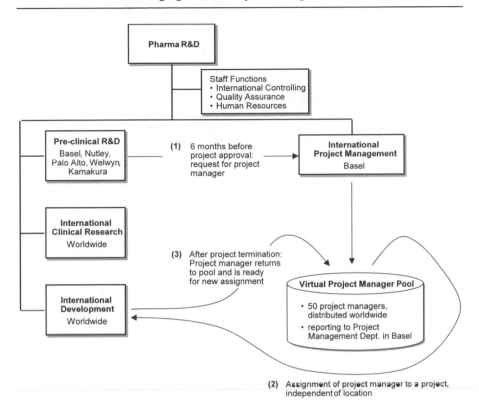

**Fig. 47.** Project management department as a virtual project management pool.

Since this new department reports directly to the board, the internal position of R&D project managers is improved. The original director of the 'International Project Management Department' was the wife of the then R&D director at board level. The establishment of a project manager pool is a clear signal for empowering one of the scarcest competitive resources. Roche manages to retain much of the valuable procedural know-how of how to conduct and lead international projects. Not only is this done on a project level, but is also placed in a position where it can be reapplied when needed. Project offices are especially valuable when projects are very long, sometimes up to 15 years as in the pharmaceutical industry. No individual is able to carry out more than 2 or 3 projects. In a project office one can learn from dozens of projects.

The director of the 'International Project Management Department' is also a member of the International Project Committee, which decides over the roughly 60 global R&D projects at Roche Pharma. The director assumes a role as interpreter or liaison between project managers and top management, thus representing the interests of international project management at Roche. This virtual pool promotes the project management idea: experienced project managers are dispersed around the world and move from project to project – no matter where the project will be conducted.

A successful human resource management approach creates an environment where every employee in R&D asks himself what his or her contribution could be across all levels of the R&D process. This approach may require abandoning the structured linear process and move towards more group- and team-oriented R&D work. Feedback loops (i.e. from the clinical trials back to basic research and the screening stages) have to be established. Post-project reviews identify not only technical but also managerial areas of improvement. The overall goal of R&D should not be to be innovative but to generate products that are successful on the market.

In addition, human resources has an obligation to develop future project managers and business leaders. Human resources should act as a consultant to department heads and group managers how to best develop and promote talented subordinates. Exit interviews still focus too much on the past and too little on improvements for future positions and future successors. Where human resources faces resistance from conservative functional managers, they should insist on the greater picture of developing motivated and educated individuals rather than stagnating technical functionaries (who are likely to leave the company for a competitor who may offer a better career path). Strategic human resource management in pharmaceuticals addresses these issues upfront, and develops a career roadmap for talented individuals who can grow through R&D projects, business development, as well as marketing and sales experience, in order to become the future R&D leaders that pharmaceutical companies need ten to fifteen years from now.

## Conclusions

Managers of pharmaceutical R&D are confronted with increased pressure regarding improvements in the number of new drugs and their respective clinical profiles, as well as concerns over cost reductions and speed in the R&D process. Key success factors for meeting these challenges are: to have the right people in the right organization working on the right projects. Escalating R&D costs are compensated by increased outsourcing of non-core activities and a clear concentration on commercial activities.

---

**Balancing R&D and Commercialization**

For many years, Pfizer was known for its successful approach to combine the best of both R&D and commercial skills. While other pharmaceutical companies can claim to be more innovative than Pfizer based on R&D-to-sales ratio comparisons, Pfizer's powerful marketing and sales machinery was able to able match its innovative capabilities with appropriate channels to bring innovations quickly to the market. Most other pharmaceutical companies used to focus more narrowly on research and development.

To be successful in the pharmaceutical market it is important to establish a balanced combination and alignment of R&D and sales. The goal of any pharmaceutical company should be to be as strong in marketing and sales as in research and development.

---

Effective knowledge management becomes more important. Knowledge is no longer restricted to research, such as information on active substances, but also includes knowledge about the important players in the scientific community as well as knowledge about potential cooperation partners or acquisition candidates in the early innovation phase. The most efficient knowledge transfer mechanism of complex know-how is through moving people: Know-how travels with heads. Blueprints are not enough. Job rotation promotes transfer of tacit knowledge.

In the increasingly complex project environment, expertise is no longer sufficient for successful project management. Instead, professionalism in project management is a must for pharmaceutical companies. Companies are trying to meet this challenge with project oriented incentive systems (e.g., dual career ladders), strong project organizations (e.g., heavy-weight-project-manager), virtual project manager pools (e.g., Roche), or novel approaches to licensing (e.g., Novartis).

Managing the entire portfolio of different projects at various stages of the product pipeline is the key to successful R&D management. A clear focus on each project's commercial potential requires the establishment of a business-oriented mindset throughout the entire pipeline including the early research and discovery stages. Human resource activities are becoming increasingly critical. Strong motivation, clear incentive systems and a culture that supports innovation are a necessity.

# VII. Future Directions and Trends

*"When it comes to R&D, we must recognize that many of the good opportunities have been picked off already and that the new opportunities are increasingly hard to find and very risky. This will be perhaps the biggest challenge for our industry in sustaining product flow."*

Fred Hassan,
Chairman, CEO and President, Schering-Plough

Improving the flow of innovation and closing the productivity gap in research and development are the foremost challenges in the pharmaceutical industry and represent the single-most important direction for future activities in pharmaceutical innovation. Given some major technological changes in drug design and delivery, the pharmaceutical industry is facing nothing short of a revolution. This final chapter identifies some trends and suggests potential future directions in leading pharmaceutical innovation:

- **Prepare for accelerating importance of open innovation.** Today's companies already rely on vast networks with various types of external partners to improve the performance of their R&D departments. This will be even more pronounced in the future. Partnerships will be created that go far beyond the well known 'technology sourcing' strategies represented by the early pharma-biotech alliances. Intensive competition, access to markets, scarce own resources, lack of know-how, cost cutting or re-structuring, growth aspirations, synergies and efficiencies, and last but not least risk reduction represent the foremost reasons why pharmaceutical companies increasingly engage in R&D activities with external partners.

- **Re-define the traditional pharmaceutical business model.** In the future, there will be fewer and fewer companies with more and more blockbusters. But diseases will also become increasingly more complex to treat. Hence, it is important to determine if the traditional paradigm of the blockbuster concept is still applicable for treating or preventing the more complex diseases. Pharmaceutical companies will not be able to rely on a few blockbuster products anymore. Personalized medicine, dependant on the genetic profiles of the patients, is required. However, people share about 99 percent identical DNA; the remaining 1 percent of differing DNA provides the opportunity for tailor-made drugs. Existing products could then be customized. Economic consequences of the resulting patient segmentation and product customization have to be considered. New business models are required. For instance, even a single compound can create its own market these days.

- **Commercialize internal research results more strategically.** A more strategic approach to improve the R&D pipeline goes along with a more aggressive commercialization of research results. Pharmaceutical companies should not only actively look for potential in-licensing candidates but also for out-licensing candidates coming from their own inventory of intellectual property. They should actively create and customize bundles of intellectual property that can subsequently be marketed to potential licensees. Due to the increasing number of niche-markets, specialty pharmaceutical companies are tempted to acquire late stage projects without having the opportunity costs and risks at earlier stages, there are several potential licensees that may have a particular need for the pharmaceutical company's intellectual assets. The pharmaceutical company should not only regard these licensees as potential competitors who possibly 'steal' blockbuster revenues. Instead, these firms should be treated as customers and partners who help generate additional revenues and profits.

- **Balance quality and volatility of the product pipeline.** The quality of the product pipeline needs to be constantly improved while the volatility of the product pipeline has to be reduced. Genuinely innovative products have a higher potential to deliver growth and shareholder value than patent defense of existing products. In addition, volatility in new product releases has a direct impact on the overall cost of capital of the corporation.

- **Complement R&D with marketing capabilities.** A stronger market-orientation in R&D is one of the primary tasks for all future R&D activities. This in turn requires a stronger business orientation of research managers and key scientists. Many scientists in pharmaceutical R&D still know too little about the markets that their products are expected to serve. A clear communication of the business benefits to the scientists is necessary. As a consequence, an effective and collaborative interface between R&D and marketing must be established. Ultimately, a stronger market-orientation is expected to result in a shift from a product- to a patient-driven strategy.

- **Establish strategy how to benefit from scientific breakthroughs.** The more we understand the human genome, the more validated biological targets will be available that will be starting points for new drug development. It is expected that the number of targets will increase by a factor of more than 20 to over 10,000 targets in the near future. The integration of genomics, proteomics, molecular design, and other technologies will lead to improved target identification and attrition, enhanced lead optimization, improved clinical trial designs that speed approval, and signal a shift from broadly targeted drugs to more focused medicines with much higher therapeutic value for the target population. With access to genomics technologies estimated to require a minimum US$ 100 million annual commitment, top-tier pharmaceutical companies are likely to be the first to fully integrate the new technologies.
- **Abandon disease-centered approach and apply a systematic concept in early discovery stages.** A wide range of other novel drug discovery technologies already in use that go beyond high-throughput screening, combinatorial chemistry or bioinformatics, and increasingly center around molecular drug design are expected to improve pharmaceutical research. The application of these technologies allows for the automation of much of the discovery function, promoting a more comprehensive and consistent screening process as well as enhancements in R&D productivity. This means a move away from a disease-centered to a systematic and mechanistic discovery process in the early phases. As a result, both the quality and quantity of resulting lead compounds are expected to increase.
- **Reduce serendipity in discovery by balancing data generation and data analysis tools.** The increasing deployment of information technologies has resulted in huge amounts of data being generated day-by-day. After the development of new information production techniques new information management techniques are required. Advanced database technologies, faster algorithms and improved statistical analyses are necessary to efficiently screen through vast quantities of information possibly eliminating at some point the reliance on serendipity alone for future successes.
- **Focus on complexity and diversity in compound libraries.** Besides applying more advanced screening methodologies, the quality of the substances that are to be screened also has to improve. Therefore, the structural complexity and diversity of the compound libraries must increase. This ultimately allows raising the probability to find a substance that is able to influence a certain target in the desired way.

- **Enhance people development.** People are at the center of any organization, thus improved people development and training will result in better run companies. Pharmaceutical companies will have to overcome the distance between early-stage research and the final product by adapting their incentive and job assignment systems. Not every scientist wants to do a stint in marketing, but every researcher should have had the exposure to the rest of the business and the opportunity to pursue a modern, more flexible career.

- **Challenge R&D employees.** All employees in R&D should ask themselves what their contribution could be across all levels of the R&D process. This approach should eliminate the linear structured process and move towards more group- and team-oriented R&D. Feedback loops (i.e. from the clinical trials back to basic research and the screening stages) must be proactively pursued.

- **Merge functional and therapeutic knowledge.** An oftentimes mentioned concern in pharmaceutical R&D is the fact that people do not interact enough with each other. Modern drug discovery requires the integration of knowledge from a broad array of disciplines. The formation of multidisciplinary teams, including biologists, physiologists, biochemists, as well as specialists in the traditional disciplines of synthetic chemistry and pharmacology, and more esoteric specialists like molecular kineticists is a necessity. Marketing experts should be included as early in the R&D process as possible. The most successful pharmaceutical companies differentiate themselves by actively confronting the tension between an organization by function and an organization by product group.

- **Balance scale and creativity.** It has been shown that creativity in pharmaceutical R&D is most likely to occur in smaller teams. The trend towards mega-mergers and ever larger companies endangers R&D's ability to be creative. Hence, with any acquisition and/or integration of outside knowledge into the inside portfolio, which is expected to be a major driver for improvement in R&D in the future, there is the potential loss of creativity and the occurrence of the not-invented-here syndrome. Embedded small functional units within the larger unit are expected to be a successful approach against these negative consequences.

- **Fail often to succeed sooner.** It is more economical and productive to terminate less prospective projects and concentrate resources on objectively more promising ones. There is a cut-off after which project management gives discipline absolute priority over incremental improvements. Before this cut-off, the R&D organization should be designed for maximal creativity and effectiveness of its discovery effort. Overall, the combined thrust of all project activities determines a company's competence areas and thus therapeutic fields.

- **Find the 'sweet spot' in the pharmaceutical value chain.** Reduced efficiency and flexibility, difficulties to transfer know-how and an unclear intellectual property situation are seen as major disadvantages in pharmaceutical R&D. Service providers, which could complement the competencies of the pharmaceutical company, may take over an increasingly important role in managing pharmaceutical innovation. Regarding the pharmaceutical company, the balance between in-house and external activities (make-or-buy decision) is mostly competency or know-how driven and not capacity or cost driven. Preferred partnerships and cooperation on a project-by-project basis with pre-selected vendors are the two most favorable cooperation models in practice. However, controlling the critical components in the value chain remains the key issue.

- **Remember that drugs solve global problems.** Pharmaceutical products can be applied everywhere in the world. Hence, R&D has also to adopt an increasingly internationalized strategy. Foremost, it is important to align the R&D strategy with corporate strategy. Is global R&D a consequence of business decisions, or is global business a consequence of R&D decisions? In this regard, it is essential to clarify what decision criteria exist and which criteria would influence the initial mission, ramp-up and evaluation of new R&D sites. Company-wide knowledge management and information and communication technologies play a critical role in the overall internationalization process.

The declining R&D productivity has led to intense criticism of pharmaceutical R&D managers. The pharmaceutical industry relies on predictable production of new medicines and therapies. While we have found many threats and dangers that imperil the prospects of any single company, the overall industry is looking forward to an exciting future. Several new technologies in the drug discovery process are in their infancy and are expected to revolutionize the way pharmaceutical companies manage innovation.

In addition, many novel markets driven by the aging population in established markets as well as by the growing population in emerging markets represent many untapped opportunities. The incorporation of market-oriented aspects, improved human resource and project leadership, better R&D pipeline management including a balanced approach to outsourcing and collaborations as well as a sound internationalization strategy are major elements in a general strategy towards prosperity for tomorrow's most successful pharmaceutical companies.

# Bibliography

Accenture (2001a): High Performance Drug Discovery – An Operating Model for a New Era. Executive Briefing. Accenture Report.

Accenture (2001b): R&D and the Internet. Accenture Report.

Accenture (2002): Commercial and R&D: Reinventing the relationship. Pharmaceuticals & medical products. Accenture White Paper.

Agarwal, S.; Desai, S.; Holcomb, M.M.; Oberoi, A. (2001): Unlocking the Value in Big Pharma. The McKinsey Quarterly, 2001, No. 2.

Albers, S.; Eggers, S. (1991): Organisatorische Gestaltungen von Produktinnovations-Prozessen. Führt der Wechsel des Organisationsgrades zu Innovationserfolg? Zeitschrift für Betriebswirtschaftliche Forschung, Vol. 43, Iss. 1, pp. 44-64.

Arthur D. Little (2003): Aktuelle Trends bei Buyouts in der Chemie- und Pharmaindustrie. Market Study, January 2003.

Arthur D. Little, Solvias (2002): External Synthesis Services for Research and Development in the Pharmaceutical Industry. Market Study, June 2002.

BAK (2001): Garant und Motor für Produktivität und Wohlstand in der Schweiz – Bedeutung der chemisch/pharmazeutischen Industrie für die Schweizer Volkswirtschaft. Baseler Konjunkturforschung: Basel.

Baumann (2003): The Challenge of Innovation in the Drug Discovery Process. Presentation at CTO-Roundtable 'Management of Pharmaceutical R&D in Turbulent Times – Perspectives and Trends'. Zurich, March 2003.

BCG (2001): A Revolution in R&D – How Genomics and Genetics are Transforming the Biopharmaceutical Industry. BCG Report: Boston, MA.

Becker, S.; Kellermann, C.; Menz, W.; Sablowski, T. (1999): Struktur und Vernetzung der Biotechnologie-Industrie. Arbeitsbericht des Projektes „Vernetzung als Wettbewerbsfaktor". Johann Wolfgang Goethe Universität, Frankfurt/Main.

Booz Allen & Hamilton (1997): In Vivo, Making Combinatory Chemistry Pay. Booz Allen & Hamilton Report: New York.

Borgulya, P. (2000): F.Hoffmann-La Roche: Global Differentiation between R and D. In: Boutellier, R.; Gassmann, O.; von Zedtwitz, M. (Editors): Managing Global Innovation. 2nd edition. Heidelberg: Springer, pp. 236-248.

Boutellier, R.; Gassmann, O.; von Zedtwitz, M. (1999): Managing Global Innovation: Uncovering the Secrets of Future Competitiveness. 2nd ed., Springer: Berlin, Tokyo, New York.

BPI (1999): Die 'Innovationsschere' der pharmazeutischen Industrie. Taken from Prof. Homburg & Partner (2001): Trends und Chancen in der Pharma-Branche. Mannheim, April 2001.

Brueckner, M.; Philipp, M.P.; and Luithle, J.E. (2005): China's Pharmaceutical Market: Business Environment and Market Dynamics. In: Festel, G.; Kreimeyer, A.; Oels, U.; von Zedtwitz, M. (2005, Editors): The Chemical and Pharmaceutical Industry in China – Challenges and Threats for Foreign Companies. Springer: Heidelberg, pp. 91-107.

Buchanan, I.P.M. (2002): R&D Collaborations – a Partners' Perspective. Vertex Pharmaceuticals. Presentation held in Zurich on 27 February 2002.

Buderi, R; Weber, J.; Hoots, C.; Neff, R. (1991): A Tighter Focus for R&D. Business Week, 2 December 1991, pp. 80-84.

Budworth, D.W. (1996): Finance and Innovation. New York.

Cantwell, J. (1995): The Globalisation of Technology: What Remains of the Product Cycle Model? In: Cambridge Journal of Economics, Vol. 19, pp. 155-174.

Cap Gemini Ernst & Young (2001): Perspectives on life science. Issue 3.

CDER (2002): Center for Drug Evaluation and Research at FDA: http://www.fda.gov/cder/, accessed September 2002.

Chen, W. (2004): Looking For an Industry Cure. China International Business, Issue 204, 34-37.

Chesbrough, H. (2003): Open Innovation: The New Imperative for Creating and Profiting from Technology. Harvard Business School Press: Boston, MA.

Chesbrough, H. (2006): Open Business Models: How to Thrive in the New Innovation Landscape. Harvard Business School Press: Boston, MA.

Dalton, D.H.; Serapio, M.G. (1995): Globalizing Industrial Research and Development. Washington, D.C.: U.S. Department of Commerce.

Datamonitor (2003): Licensing Strategies: Benchmarking Analysis of the Top 20 Pharmaceutical Companies. April 2003, p. 52.

Davis, S.; Botkin, J. (1994): The Coming of Knowledge-Based Business. Harvard Business Review, 5, pp. 165-170.

Deck, M.; Strom, M. (2002): Model of Co-development Emerges. In: Research Technology Management, May-June, pp. 47-53.

De Meyer, A. (1991): Tech Talk: How Managers Are Stimulating Global R&D Communication. In: Sloan Management Review, 32, 3, pp. 49-58.

DiMasi, J. (2001): Tufts Center for the Study of Drug Development Pegs Costs of a New Prescription Drug at $802 Million. Press release, Tufts University, 30 November 2001.

Economiesuisse (2006): F+E in der Schweizerischen Privatwirtschaft. Zürich.

Ernst&Young (2002): Beyond Borders – The Global Biotechnology Report 2002. Global Health Sciences. Ernst&Young Report.

Federal Social Insurance Office (2002): http://www.bsv.admin.ch/, accessed September 2002.

Federal Statistical Office (1998): Costs of Public Health Care. Bern. http://www.statistik.admin.ch/, accessed September 2002.

Federal Statistical Office (1999): Costs of Public Health Care. Bern. http://www.statistik.admin.ch/, accessed February 2003.

Festel, G.; Polastro, E. (2002): Dritte arbeiten häufig kostengünstiger. In: Chemische Rundschau, Vol. 55, No. 13, 28 June 2002, p. 7.

Freudenheim, M.; Peterson, M. (2001): The Drug-Price Express Runs into a Wall. In: The New York Times, 23 December 2001, p. 3.

Gassmann, O. (1997): Internationales F&E-Management – Potentiale und Gestaltungskonzepte transnationaler F&E-Projekte. Oldenbourg: München, Wien.

Gassmann, O. (2001): E-Technologien in dezentralen Innovationsprozessen. Zeitschrift für Betriebswirtschaft, Supplementary Edition 3/2001, pp. 73-90.

Gassmann, O. (2006): Opening up the Innovation Process: Towards an Agenda. In: R&D Management, Vol. 36, No. 3, pp. 223-226.

Gassmann, O.; Han, Z. (2004): Motivations and Barriers of Foreign R&D Activities in China. In: R&D Management, Vol. 34, No. 4, pp. 423-437.

Gassmann, O.; Keupp M.M. (2007): The Competitive Advantage of Early and Rapidly Internationalising SMEs in the Biotechnology Industry: A Knowledge Based View. In: Journal of World Business, Special Issue: The Early and Rapid Internationalisation of the Firm, Vol. 42, pp. 350-366.

Gassmann, O.; von Zedtwitz, M. (1998): Organization of Industrial R&D on a Global Scale. In: R&D Management, Vol. 28, No. 3, pp. 147-161.

Gassmann, O.; von Zedtwitz, M. (1999): New Concepts and Trends in International R&D Organization. In: Research Policy, Vol. 28, pp. 231-250.

Gassmann, O.; von Zedtwitz, M. (2003): Trends and Determinants of Managing Virtual R&D Teams. In: R&D Management, Vol. 33, No. 3, pp. 243-262.

Gassmann, O.; Reepmeyer, G. (2003): Innovationspotentiale im Successful Ageing in der Schweiz. Unpublished report conducted for the Swiss Federal Office for Professional Education and Technology. Bern.

Gassmann, O.; Reepmeyer, G. (2006): Wachstumsmarkt Alter, Innovationen für die Zielgruppe 50+, Hanser: München, Wien.

Gassmann, O.; Reepmeyer, G.; von Zedtwitz, M.; (2003): Analyzing Structures of the Pharmaceutical Industry in Switzerland. In: Journal of Health Care and Society, Vol. 13, No. 2.

Grabowski, H.; Vernon, J.; DiMasi, J.; (2002): Returns on Research and Development for 1990s New Drug Introductions. In: Pharmacoeconomics 20, Suppl. 3 (December 2002), pp. 11-29.

Greis, N.P.; Dibner, M.D.; Bean, A.S. (1995): External Partnering as a Response to Innovation Barriers and Global Competition in Biotechnology. In: Research Policy, Vol. 24, pp. 609-630.

Gueth, A. (2001): Entering into an Alliance with Big Pharma. Benchmarks for Drug Delivery Contract Service Providers. In: Pharmaceutical Technology, October 2001, pp. 132-135.

Handelszeitung (2002): Pharmamarkt wächst rasant. Handelszeitung, No. 16, 17 April 2002, p. 1.

Herrling, P.L. (1998): Maximizing Pharmaceutical Research by Collaboration. In: Nature, Vol. 392, Supp. 30 April 1998, pp. 32-35.

Hofmann, D. (1997): Das virtuelle Unternehmen. Neue Zürcher Zeitung, 25 October 1997, p. 29.

Hofstede, G. (1980): Culture's Consequences: International Differences in Work Related Values. Beverly Hills.

Homburg & Partner (2001): Trends und Chancen in der Pharma-Branche. Mannheim, April 2001.

Houston, J.G.; Banks, M. (1997): The Chemical-Biological Interface: Developments in Automated and Miniaturised Screening Technology. In: Current Opinion in Biotechnology, 8, pp. 734-740.

IBM Business Consulting Services (2003): A Survey of Strategic Licensing Practices in the Pharmaceutical Industry. IBM Institute for Business Value Executive Brief, accessed at: http://www.ibm.com/bcs.

IHA-IMS (2002): http://www.ihaims.ch, accessed September 2002.

IHA-IMS Health (2002): Taken from Handelszeitung (2002): Pharmamarkt wächst rasant. Handelszeitung, No. 16, 17 April 2002, p. 1.

IMS Health (2000): Pharmaceutical Pricing Update. Taken from PhRMA (2001): http://www.phrma.org, including information updated in 2001, accessed on 31 March 2003.

Intercantonal Office for the Control of Medicines (Interkantonale Kontrollstelle für Heilmittel (2002): Public Information, http://www.iks.ch, accessed September 2002.

Interpharma (2001): Pharma-Markt Schweiz. Basel.

Jaikumar, R.; Upton, D.M. (1993): The Coordination of Global Manufacturing. In: Bradley, P.; Hausman, J.; Nolan, R. (Eds.): Globalization, Technology, and Competition, Harvard Business School Press: Boston MA.

Jakob, R. (2003): Eines von 47 Biotechunternehmen hat ein erfolgreiches Produkt. In: New Management, No. 3, pp. 10-13.

Kollmer, H.; Dowling, M. (2004): Licensing as a Commercialisation Strategy for New Technology-based Firms. In: Research Policy, Vol. 33, pp. 1141-1151.

KPMG (2002): Pharmaceuticals – Global Insights. By John Morris, Chair of the Europe, Middle East, South Asia, Africa Chemicals & Pharmaceuticals Practice. KPMG Report, February 2002.

La Merie (2007): R&D Pipeline News: Blockbuster Drugs 2006. July 6, 2007: http://www.pipelinereview.com, accessed September 2007.

Lehman Brothers (1999): Pharmaceutical Outsourcing Digest. 3 December 1999.

Leutenegger, J.-M. (1994): Wettbewerbsorientierte Informationssysteme in der Schweizer Pharma-Branche.

Lichtenberg, F. (1996): The Effect of Pharmaceutical Utilization and Innovation on Hospitalization and Mortality. National Bureau of Economic Research.

Lichtenberg, F. (2000): Are the Benefits of Newer Drugs Worth Their Costs? Evidence from the 1996 MEPS. In: Health Affairs, 20, 5, p. 241.

Lin, B.-W. (2001): Strategic Alliances and Innovation Networks in the Biopharmaceutical Industry. Institute of Technology Management, National Tsinghua University, Hsinchu, Taiwan.

Liu, C.X. and Xiao, P.G. (2002): Recalling the Research and Development of New Drugs Originating from Chinese Traditional and Herbal Drugs. In: Asian Journal of Drug Metabolism and Pharmacokinetics 2 (2), pp. 133-156.

MedAdNews (2000): MedAd News, November 2000, as cited in: Accenture (2002): Commercial and R&D: Reinventing the relationship. Pharmaceuticals & medical products. Accenture White Paper.

MedAdNews (2007): Top 50 Pharmaceutical Companies, MedAdNews, September 2007.

Megantz, R.C. (2002): Technology Management – Developing and Implementing Effective Licensing Programs. New York: John Wiley and Sons.

Mueller, B. (2000): Schering: Synchronised Drug Development. In: Boutellier, R.; Gassmann, O.; von Zedtwitz, M. (Editors): Managing Global Innovation. 2$^{nd}$ edition. Heidelberg: Springer, pp. 249-257.

National Science Board (1996): Science & Engineering Indicators – 1996, NSB 96-21. Washington D.C.: U.S. Government Printing Office.

Nefiodow, L.A. (1990): Der fünfte Kontradieff, Frankfurt.

Newman, D.J.; Cragg, G.M.; Snader, K.M. (2003): Natural Products as Sources of New Drugs over the Period 1981-2002. In: Journal of Nat. Prod. 66, pp. 1022-1037.

Nightingale, P. (2000): Economies of Scale in Experimentation: Knowledge and Technology in Pharmaceutical R&D. In: Industrial and Corporate Change, 9, 2, pp. 315-359.

Nonaka, I.; Takeuchi, H. (1995): The Knowledge-Creating Company. How Japanese Companies Create the Dynamics of Innovation. Oxford: New York.

NZZ (2002): Der Novartis-Hauptsitz bleibt in Basel. Neue Zürcher Zeitung, 16 May 2002, p. 29.

OECD (1999): OECD Health Data. http://www.oecd.org/statistics, accessed September 2002.

OECD (2000): OECD Health Data. http://www.oecd.org/statistics, accessed February 2003.

OECD (2002): Science, Technology and Industry Outlook: Drivers of Growth: Information Technology, Innovation, and Entrepreneurship. Special Issue of the STI Outlook. OECD, Paris.

Paetz, O; Reepmeyer, G. (2003): F&E-Allianzen in der Arzneimittelentwicklung. Paper presented at Doctoral Seminar at the University of St. Gallen. June 2003, St. Gallen.

Pearce, R.D.; Singh, S. (1990): The Internationalisation of Research and Development by Multinational Enterprises: A Firm-level Analysis of Determinants. No. 145, GB-Whiteknights.

Pharma Information (2001): Swiss Health Care and Pharmaceutical Market. Edition 2001. Interpharma: Basel.

Pharma Information (2002): Swiss Health Care and Pharmaceutical Market. Edition 2002. Interpharma: Basel.

Pfeiffer, P. (2000): Sicherung von F&E-Kompetenz in multinationalen Pharmaunternehmen. Dissertation at the University of St. Gallen, Dissertation-No. 2362.

Pfiffner, M.; Stadelmann, P.D. (1995): Arbeit und Management in der Wissensgesellschaft. Dissertation at the University of St. Gallen.

Pfizer (1999): The Pfizer Journal, Vol. 3, Iss. 2.

PhRMA (2001): http://www.phrma.org, including information updated in 2001, accessed on 31 March 2003.

PhRMA (2002): Pharmaceutical Research and Manufacturers of America. Industry Profile 2002.

PhRMA (2003): Pharmaceutical Research and Manufacturers of America, PhRMA Annual Membership Survey.

PhRMA (2004): Pharmaceutical Research and Manufacturers of America. Industry Profile 2004.

PhRMA (2007): Pharmaceutical Research and Manufacturers of America. Industry Profile 2007.

Porter, M. E. (1985): Competitive Advantage: Creating and Sustaining Superior Performance. Macmillan: New York.

Recombinant Capital (2005): Analyst's Notebook. Trends. http://www.recap.com/ consulting.nsf/ANB_tab_trends?openform, accessed 11 February 2005.

Reepmeyer, G. (2005): Risk-sharing in the Pharmaceutical Industry – The Case of Out-licensing. Physica-Verlag: Heidelberg.

Reuters (2002): Pharmaceutical Innovation – An Analysis of Leading Companies and Strategies. Reuters Business Insight, Healthcare.

Reuters (2003a): The Blockbuster Drug Outlook to 2007: Identifying, Creating and Maintaining the Pharmaceutical Industry's Growth Drivers. Reuters Business Insight, Healthcare.

Reuters (2003b): Patent Protection Strategies: Maximizing Market Exclusivity. Reuters Business Insight, Healthcare.

Reuters (2003c): Pharmaceutical R&D Outsourcing Strategies – An Analysis of Market Drivers and Resistors to 2010. Reuters Business Insight, Healthcare.

Robbins-Roth, C. (2001): Zukunftsbranche Biotechnologie. Gabler.

Rothaermel, F.T. (2001): Complemetary Assets, Strategic Alliances, and the Incumbent's Advantage: An Empirical Study of Industry and Firm Effects in the Biopharmaceutical Industry. In: Research Policy, Vol. 30, pp. 1235-1251.

Saftlas, H. (2001): Industry Surveys, Healthcare: Pharmaceuticals. Standard & Poors: New York, 27 December 2001, p. 32.

Savioz, P. (2002): Technology Intelligence in Technology-based SMEs – Conceptual Design and Implementation. Zürich.

Schlatter, R. (2002): Pharmamarkt wächst rasant. Handelszeitung, No. 16, 17 April 2002, p. 8.

Shane, S. (1992): Why do Some Societies Invent more than Others? In: Journal of Business Venturing, 7, pp. 29-46.

Shane, S. (1993): Cultural Influences on National Rates of Innovation. In: Journal of Business Venturing, 8, pp. 59-73.

Speedel (2004): Introducing the Speedel Group. Company presentation. http://www.speedelgroup.com, accessed on 10 September 2004.

SSCI (2000): http://www.sgci.ch, accessed September 2002.

SSCI (2002): http://www.sgci.ch, accessed September 2002.

Standort Schweiz (2003): Biotechnology http://www.standortschweiz.ch/seco/ internet/en/technologies/biotechnology/index.html, accessed 3 February 2003.

Swissmedic (2002): http://www.swissmedic.ch, accessed September 2002.

Swiss Scientific Council (1999): Fakten & Bewertungen 4/99. In: Pharma Information (2002); based upon Science, Vol. 725, 7 February 1997.

Thiel, K.A. (2004): Good-bye Columbus! New NRDOs forego discovery. In: Nature Biotechnology, Vol. 22, No. 9, pp. 1087-1092.

Thurow, L. (1996): The Future of Capitalism. Penguin.

VIPS (2002): Arzneitmittelmarkt Schweiz 2001: Wachstum durch innovative Arzneimittel. In: VIPS, Pharma Direkt, No. 13, March 2002.

von Zedtwitz, M. (1999): Managing Interfaces in International R&D. Dissertation at the University of Gallen, Dissertation-No. 2315.

von Zedtwitz, M.; Gassmann, O. (2002): Market versus Technology Drive in R&D Internationalization: Four Different Patterns of Managing Research and Development. In: Research Policy, 31, 4, pp. 569-588.

von Zedtwitz, M.; Gassmann, O.; Reepmeyer, G.; (2003): Managing Pharmaceutical R&D – The Case of Switzerland. R&D Management Conference, Manchester, July 2003.

Völker, R. (1999): Wertorientiertes Controlling der Produktentwicklung. Kostenrechnungspraxis, 43, 1999, 4, pp. 201-208.

Völker, R. (2001): Planung und Steuerung von Entwicklungsprojekten in der Pharmabranche. In: Gassmann, O.; Kobe, C.; Voit, E. (Eds.): High-Risk-Projekte. Springer: Berlin, Heidelberg, New York, pp. 231-247.

Wang, A.; von Zedtwitz, M. (2005): Developing the Pharmaceutical Business in China – the Case of Novartis. In: Festel, G.; Kreimeyer, A.; Oels, U.; von Zedtwitz, M. (Eds.): The Chemical and Pharmaceutical Industry in China – Challenges and Threats for Foreign Companies. Springer: Heidelberg. 109-119.

Webber, D.E. (2005): China's Approach to Innovative Pharmaceutical R&D: a Review. In: Festel, G.; Kreimeyer, A.; Oels, U.; von Zedtwitz, M. (Eds.): The Chemical and Pharmaceutical Industry in China – Challenges and Threats for Foreign Companies. Springer: Heidelberg. 121-131.

West, J. (1998): Building a High-Performing Team. In: Cleland, D. (Ed.): Field Guide to Project Management. Wiley: New York, pp. 239-254.

WGZ Bank (2002): Branchenanalyse Life Science. WGZ Report, Oktober 2002. Düsseldorf.

Whittaker, E.; Bower, D. J. (1994): A Shift to External Alliances for Product Development in the Pharmaceutical Industry. In: R&D Management, Vol. 24, No. 3, pp. 249-260.

Windhover (2000): Opportunism Knocks. Windhover's Review of Emerging Medical Ventures. Vol. 5, No. 4, pp. 32. http://www.windhover.com/ contents/monthly/exex/e_2000900064.htm, accessed on 19 December 2004.

Windhover (2003): In-licensing: Still a difficult model. Windhover's Review of Emerging Medical Ventures. Vol. 8, No. 10. http://www.windhover.com/ contents/monthly/exex/e_2003900172.htm, accessed on 19 December 2004.

Wood Mackenzie (2003a): As cited in presentation by F. Humer, CEO of Roche, June 2003.

Wood Mackenzie (2003b): As cited in company presentation by Speedel, February 2004.

WTO (2002): http://www.wto.org, accessed 18 February 2003.

Zambrowicz, B.P.; Sands, A.T. (2003): Knockouts Model The 100 Best-Selling Drugs – Will They Model The Next 100? In: Nature Reviews Drug Discovery, 2, January 2003, pp. 38-51.

Zanetti, P.; Steiner, U. (2001): Sektorstudie Pharma Europa – Biotech als Hoffnungsträger. Leu Investment Research: Zürich.

Zeller, C. (2001): Globalisierungsstrategien – der Weg von Novartis. Springer: Heidelberg.

# Index

3M, *105*

ABB, *103, 104, 105*
Abbott, *5, 6, 7, 8, 13*, 65
Actelion, *144*
Active Pharmaceutical Ingredient
    (API), 179
Active substance, synthesis, 62
Acute toxicity, 63
Administration, 93
Advair, 7
AHP, *109*
Akzo Nobel, *105*
Alcatel, *105*
Aliskiren, 137, 142
Altana, *84*
Alvesco, 84
ALZA, *152*
Amgen, *5, 6, 7, 8, 13*, 34, *52*
Antagonist-model, 130
Aranesp, 7
Astra, *14*
AstraZeneca, *5, 6, 7, 8, 13, 14, 109,
    115*
Attrition rate, 51
Avapro, 82
Aventis, *5, 6, 8, 14*, 75, 84, 85, 93,
    94
Axys Pharmaceuticals, *24*

Balance of power, 23
Bargaining power
    of buyers, 23, 25
    of suppliers, 23, 24
BASF, *61*, 65, 67, *105*
Basilea Pharmaceutica, *123*

Baxter, *13*
Bayer, *5, 6, 7, 8, 13*, 61, 80, 83, 86,
    87, 92, *105*, 133, *135*, 136, *154*
Biochips, 179
Biogen, *5, 6, 7, 8*
Bioinformatics, 37, 40, 161, 179
Biomedical institutions, *113*
Bioprocessing, 179
Biotechnology, 1, 24, 33–38, 48,
    107, 132, 149
Biotechnology research institutes,
    *113*
BioXell, *123, 144*
Blockbuster drug, ix, 4, 5, 7, 9, 18,
    28, 44, 52, 68, 108, 128, 159, 179
BMS, 7
Boehringer Ingelheim, *13, 109*, 152
Bosch, *105*
Bristol-Myers Squibb, *5, 6, 8, 13,
    14*, 82
Byk Gulden, *84*

Call-back option, 93
Canon, *105*
Celera, *24*
Centers of excellence, 106
Cerberus, *105*
Chemistry, 19, 57, 59
    combinatorial, 37, 39, 161, 180
    medical, 132
    organic, 33
    synthetic, 132, 162
Chemoinformatics, 179
China, vi, 111, 112
Chinese medicines, 112
Chiron, *80*
Ciba, *14*

Clinical
    development, xi, 108
    research, 1, 24
    stages, 38
    studies, 1
    testing, human, 33
    trial data, 15
    trial design, 161
    trials, 54, 57, 63–64, 72, 74, 135,
        144, 156
Clinical profile, 15
    administration, 15
    dosage, 15
    efficacy, 15
    safety, 15
    side effects, 15
Cloning, 179
Co-development, 78, 79, 83
Commercialization process, 91, 96
Compaq, 59
Competition, potential, 26
Compliance, 92
Compound, 33, 38, 44, 58, 59, 123,
    135, 160
Compound libraries, 36, 37, 41
Compounding, 180
Computer simulations, 37
Consta, 7
Contract
    manufacturing organization
        (CMO), 72, 95, 97, 180
    research organization (CRO), 27,
        72, 180
    service organization (CSO), 72,
        180
Cooperation models, 74, 130
Cost structure, 2
Cozaar, 142
Crowdsourcing, 68
Crystallography, 47
Cultural differences, 118
Cytos, 15, 36

Daewoo, 105
DaimlerChrysler, 103

Deoxyribonucleic Acid (DNA), 43,
    160, 180
Diagnostic, 180
Dow Chemical, 105
Drug development
    clinical, 64
    costs, ix, 2
    duration, 2, 135
    pipeline, 1, 100
    pre-clinical, 63
    process, 73
Drug Development Plan, 129
Drug discovery, 56
Drug target function, 37
Drugs
    generic, 21, 181
    genetically manufactured, 22
    genomics-based, 54
    individualized, 43
    non-prescription, 21
    orphan, 22, 182
    over-the-counter (OTC), 182
    prescription, 21
    tailor-made, 160
DuPont, 105
Duragesic, 9

Efficacy, 53, 180
Eisai, 105, 109
Electrolux, 105
Elf Aquitaine, 105
Eli Lilly, 5, 6, 8, 13, 14, 21, 33, 34,
    68, 84, 86, 94, 109, 115
Enbrel, 7
Enzyme, 180
Epogen, 7, 34, 52
Ericsson, 103
Esec, 105
Experimentation, 37

Face-to-face time, 117
Factoring, 129
Feedback loops, 156, 162
Financial risk, 60
Food and Drug Administration
    (FDA), 2, 29, 180

*Ford, 105*
*Forest, 5, 6, 8*
Free-cash-flow, 66
*Fujitsu, 103, 105*
*Fulcrum-Pharma, 144*

*G.D. Searle, 152*
Gene, 180
   mapping, 181
   sequencing, 181
   splicing, xi, 181
Gene technology, 22
*Genentech, 5, 6, 13, 33, 34, 80, 84*
*General Electric, 103*
*General Motors, 103, 105*
Generics, 28, *112*
   companies, *112*
Genetic
   diseases, 181
   engineering, 47, 181
Genetics, 181
Genome sequencing, *113*
Genomic
   library, 181
   revolution, 45
Genomics, 37, 43, 161, 181
   research, *113*
*Glaxo Wellcome, v, 14, 105, 109*
*GlaxoSmithKline, 5, 6, 7, 8, 13, 14, 44, 45, 52, 82, 115*
Gleevec, 54
Glucophage, 82
Good citizen, 106
Growth, v, 12
Growth strategies, 14

Half-time of trust, 120
Health authority, 65
Hepatitis C, 152
High-throughput screening, xi, 37, 38, 161, 182
*Hitachi, 105*
*Hoechst, 14, 105*
Human genome, 161
Human Genome Project, 36, 42

Humulin, 33, 34
*Hyundai, 105*

*IBM, 105*
Immunology, 182
*Incyte, 44*
Information technologies, 41
In-licensing, 68, 78, 79, 81
InnoGel, 95
Innovation
   clusters, 146
   drivers for, 37
   scissors, 57
Insulin, 33
*Intarcia, 151*
Intellectual property, 114, 136
Intellectual property rights, 28, 133
International Development Team, 125, 126
International Drug Development System, 129
International Project Management, 126, 154
Internationalization, xi, 14, 103–21, 107, 163
Internet communication, 55
*InterPharmaLink, 95*
Investigational New Drug (IND)
   application, 182
   approval, 92
   treatment, 184

Job rotation, 154
*Johnson&Johnson, 5, 6, 7, 8, 13, 14, 34, 115*

*Kao, 105*
*King Pharmaceuticals, 93, 94*
*Kubota, 105*

Launch, 65
Lead-optimization, 47
Legal battles, vi
*Lehman Bros., 45*
*Leica Microsystems, 105*

License
  business, 136
  product, 136
  technology, 136
Licensing, 1, 123
  In-licensing, 68, 78, 79, 81
  Out-licensing, 68, 78, 79, 86, 88,
    91, 94, 98, 137
Licensing agreement, 34, 44, 99
Life science products, 20, 30
Lifecycle management, 55
Lipitor, 7, 8, 83, 114
Lipobay, 83
Local content rules, 106
Losartan, 142
Lotensin/Lotrel, 9

MabThera, 7
*Mahle, 105*
Make-or-buy decision, 163
Market
  access, 73
  entry, 16
Marketing
  model, vi
  target group, 55
  tasks, 55
*Matsushita, 105*
*Merck*, vi, *5, 6, 7, 8, 13, 14, 40, 48,*
  83, 142, *144*
*Merck KGaA*, 87
Mergers & Acquisitions (M&A), 13
Mergers, mega, 14
*Mettler-Toledo, 104, 105*
Milestone payment, 99
*Millennium*, 80, 85
Molecular
  design, 37, 47, 161
  genetics, 182
*Myriad, 44*

National healthcare, 25
*NEC, 105*
*Nestlé, 105*
Net profit margin, 23
Net-present-value method, 65

Neupogen, 34
New Chemical Entity (NCE), 182
New Drug Application (NDA), 92,
  182
New drug registration, 65
New market entrants, 26
New Molecular Entity (NME), 2,
  182
Nexium, 7
*Nippon Steel, 105*
*Nokia, 105*
Norvasc, 7
Not-invented-here syndrome, 162
*Novartis, 5, 6, 7, 8, 13, 14, 21, 44,*
  *52, 54, 66, 76, 80, 86, 103, 105,*
  *108, 109, 115, 130,* 137, 148, 157
Novartis Institute for BioMedical
  Research (NIBR), 148
*Novartis Venture Fund, 75*
*Novo Nordisk, 5, 6, 8, 105, 109, 115*
*NovoGEL, 95*

Office of Technology, 127
Omega DUROS, 152
Open innovation, vi, vii, 68, 159
Out-licensing, 68, 78, 79, 86, 88, 91,
  94, 98, 137
  contract, 140
  process, 138
Outsourcing, xi, 68, 73, 130

Patent, 51, 134
  law, 30
  protection, 30
  protection period, 135
  search, 62
Patentable invention
  composition, 134
  process, 134
  product, 134
  use, 134
*Pfizer*, v, *5, 6, 7, 8, 13, 14, 25, 27,*
  *43, 45, 68,* 83, 85, *105, 109, 115,*
  152, *157*
Pharmaceutical market
  structure, *112*

Pharmaceutical value chain, 34, 72
  disaggregation, 68
*Pharmacia*, v, *5*, *6*, *8*, *14*, 152
Pharmacodynamics, 183
Pharmacogenomics, 37, 45, 183
Pharmacokinetics, 63, 183
*Philips*, *103*, *105*
*PhRMA*, 86, 183
Pipeline management, 51–101
Planning horizon, 66
Plavix, 7, 82
Portfolio Board, 126, 127
Portfolio management, 65, 67
Pravachol, 8, 82
Pre-launch awareness, 17
Prescription price, 26
Price regulation, 28
Procrit, 7, 34
*Procter & Gamble*, *13*
Product
  lifecycle, 133
  line extension, 55
  pipeline, 160
  registration, 28
  revenues, expected, 67
  standards, 107
Product Development Board, 128
Productivity, v, xi
Productivity paradox, v, 1
Project management, 61
Project management pools, virtual,
  153
*Prometheus*, 76, 77
Promotion, pre-launch, 16
Proteomics, 37, 42, 161, 183
*Protodigm*, *144*
*Purdue*, *5*, *6*

Quality control, 65

R&D
  challenges, 58
  collaboration, *114*
  controlling, 128
  expenditures, 2, 12
    expenditures, in Switzerland, 146
    labs, locations, 110
    partnerships, 70
    performance, 1
    pipeline management, xi
    process, 58
    productivity, ix, 51
    regulations, 28
    sites, 108
    strategy, 125
R&D internationalization
  drivers, 105
  problems, 117
R&D process, phases, 59
  development, 60
  market introduction, 60
  pre-project, 60
Rampiril, 94
Rational drug design, 47
Real options, 67
Recombinant, 183
Registration, new drug, 65
Regulative force, 23, 28
Reimbursement, 93
Research alliance, 78, 79
Research and discovery, 62
Research Board, 128
Research-to-development handover,
  127
Return-on-equity, 23
*Rhone-Poulanc*, *14*, *105*
Ribonucleic Acid (RNA), 40, 43,
  183
Risperdal, 7
Rituxan, 7
*Roche*, *5*, *6*, 7, *13*, *14*, *45*, *62*, 80, 86,
  *103*, *105*, *109*, *115*, 123, 127, *128*,
  *144*, *153*, 157
*Royal Dutch/Shell*, *104*, *105*, *110*
Royalty revenues, 92, 99, 137

*Sandoz*, *14*, 27
*Sanofi-Aventis*, 7, *13*
*Sanofi-Synthélabo*, *5*, *6*, *8*
*SAP*, *105*

*Schering*, 86, 94, *105, 109*, 125, *126*, 152
*Schering-Plough*, *5, 6, 8, 13*, 19, *45*, 51, 159
*Schindler*, *105*
Scientific
    community, 106
    institutes, *113*
Screening, 63
Screening methodologies, 161
Serendipity, 39
Seretide, 7
Service provider, 74, 132, 163
Services
    development, 133
    production, 133
*Servier*, *115*
*Sharp*, *105*
*Siemens*, *105*
Site management organization (SMO), 72, 180
*SmithKline Beecham*, v, *14, 44*
Soft capsule market, 95
*Solvias*, 130, *131, 132, 133*
*Sony*, *105*
*Speedel*, 137, 142
Spill-over, ix
Stock market, ix
Substitute products, 23, 27
*Sulzer*, *105*

*Takeda*, *7, 13*
*TAP*, *5, 6, 7, 8*
Target, 62, 183
Target-profile, 66
Taxes, 73
Taxol, 82
Teams, multi-disciplinary, 154, 162
Therapies, alternative, 27
Therapy areas
    adjunct therapy, 8, 9
    arthritis pain, 9
    cardiovascular, 8, 9

central nervous system (CNS), 8, 9
diabetes, 9
gastrointestinal, 8, 9
immune disorders & inflammation, 9
infectious disease, 8, 9
oncology, 9
respiratory, 8, 9
women's health, 9
Time-to-market, 28, 127
Toxicogenomics, 184
Toxicology, 184
*Toyota*, *103, 105*
Traditional Chinese Medicines (TCM), *112*
Treatment Investigational New Drug, 184

Ultra high-throughput screening, 38
Uncertainty, 144

Vaccine, 184
Viagra, ix
Vioxx, vi
Virtual lab, 40
*Volkswagen*, *105*
*Volvo*, *105*

*Wal-Mart*, vi
*Warner-Lambert*, v, 83
Work packages, 61
*Wyeth*, *5, 6, 7, 8, 13*

*Xerox*, *105*

*Yamanouchi*, 83, *109*
Yokohama National University, x

*Zeneca*, *14*
Zocor, 8, 83

# Glossary

API (Active Pharma-
ceutical Ingredient)
: Any substance or mixture of substances intended to be used in the manufacture of a drug. When used in the production of a drug, it becomes an active ingredient of the drug product.

Biochips
: While containing DNA, Biochips are used to automate the sequencing of genes.

Bioinformatics
: The use of IT in pharmaceutical R&D (e.g., electronic databases of genomes and protein sequences, and computer modeling of biomolecules and biologic systems). Bioinformatics is expected to expedite lead discovery by providing structural data and analysis for drug targets.

Bioprocessing
: The creation of a product utilizing a living organism.

Blockbuster
: A pharmaceutical product earning annual revenues in excess of US$ 1 billion.

Chemoinformatics
: The combination of chemical synthesis, biological screening, and data mining approaches used to guide drug discovery and development.

Cloning
: Using specialized DNA technology to produce multiple, exact copies of a single gene or other segment of DNA. The resulting, cloned (copied) collections of DNA molecules are also referred to as clone libraries. A second type of cloning exploits the natural process of cell division to make many copies of an entire cell. The genetic makeup of these cloned cells, called a cell line, is identical to the original cell. A third type of cloning pro-

duces complete, genetically identical organisms (e.g., animals).

| | |
|---|---|
| Combinatorial Chemistry | It allows large numbers of compounds to be made by the systemic and repetitive covalent connection of a set of different 'building blocks' of varying structures to each other. |
| Compounding | Bringing together excipient and solvent components into a homogeneous mix of active ingredients. |
| CSO (Contract Service Organization) | Any organization that provides pharmaceutical companies with a contract service. Among others, the term CSO includes: CROs (contract research organizations), CMOs (contract manufacturing organizations), SMOs (site management organizations). |
| Diagnostic | A substance or group of substances used to identify a disease by analyzing cause and symptoms. |
| DNA (Deoxyribonucleic Acid) | DNA represents the molecular basis for genes. Every inherited characteristic has its origin somewhere in the code of an organism's complement of DNA. |
| Efficacy | The ability of a substance to produce a desired effect. |
| Enzyme | Macromolecules, mostly of protein nature, that function as (bio-) catalysts. They not only promote reactions but also function as regulators making sure the organism does not produce too much or too little of any chemical substance. |
| FDA | Food and Drug Administration (U.S. regulatory approval body for new pharmaceutical products). |
| Gene | A natural unit of hereditary material that is the physical basis for the transmission of the charac- |

teristics of living organisms from one generation to another. The basic genetic material is essentially the same in all living organisms. It consists of deoxyribonucleic acid (DNA) in most organisms and ribonucleic acid (RNA) in certain viruses.

Gene Mapping

Determination of the relative positions of genes on a DNA molecule (chromosome or plasmid) and of the distance (in linkage units or physical units) between them.

Gene Sequencing

The determination of the sequence of bases in a DNA strand.

Gene Splicing

The enzymatic attachment of one gene or part of a gene to another.

Generic Drug

Replication of a prescription or non-prescription drug where the patent protection has expired. Generic drugs (also referred to as generics) are usually offered by firms that did not develop the drugs themselves but gained a license to sell the drug.

Genetics

The study of the genetic composition, heredity, and variation of organisms.

Genetic Diseases

Diseases that occur because of a mutation in the genetic material.

Genetic Engineering

The selective, deliberate alteration of genes by technological means.

Genomics

The process of identifying genes involved in disease through the comparison of the genomes of individuals with and without disease.

Genomic Library

A collection of clones made from a set of randomly generated overlapping DNA fragments representing the entire genome of an organism.

| | |
|---|---|
| High-throughput Screening | The process for the rapid assessment of the activity of samples from a combinatorial library or other compound collection. |
| Immunology | The study of how the body defends itself against disease. |
| IND (Investigational New Drug) Application | A document filed with the FDA prior to clinical trial of a new drug. It gives a full description of the new drug, such as where and how it is manufactured. An IND permission has to be kept active annually by sending, for example, annual reports. The IND is followed by the NDA (New Drug Application). |
| Molecular Genetics | The study of the nature and biochemistry of genetic material. It includes the technologies of genetic engineering. |
| NCE (New Chemical Entity) | Referring to newly approved pharmaceutical products. |
| NDA (New Drug Application) | The process of determining the benefit-risk profile of a new drug after completion of the clinical tests and prior to approval for marketing. |
| NME (New Molecular Entity) | Referring to newly approved pharmaceutical products. |
| Orphan Drug | A drug that is believed to substantially increase the life expectancy of the treated patient for a particular disease. While developing an orphan drug, competitors are usually excluded from receiving a license to produce a similar drug for a finite period (usually 7 years), thereby allowing the company producing the drug to recuperate R&D expenses. |
| OTC (Over-the-Counter) Drug | A drug that can usually be purchased without a prescription. An OTC drug is also sometimes re- |

ferred to as a drug purely used for self-medication purposes and is typically used for minor ailments such as headache or the flu.

Pharmacodynamics          Quantitative study of drug action.

Pharmacogenomics          The study of how the response to a drug is affected by individual genetic variations. It is aimed at the prescription or development of drugs that maximize benefit and minimize side effects in individuals.

Pharmacokinetics          Quantitative study of how drugs are taken up, biologically transformed, distributed, metabolized, and eliminated from the body.

PhRMA                     Pharmaceutical Research and Manufacturers of America (an organization representing the leading research-based pharmaceutical and biotechnology companies in the US).

Proteomics                The study of the entire protein output of cells. It refers to any protein-based approach that has the capacity to provide new information about proteins on a genome-wide scale.

RNA (Ribonucleic Acid)    A single-strand molecule that partners with DNA to manufacture proteins.

Recombinant               Recombining of generic material from one species into alternate sequences.

Target                    The target molecule is usually responsible for causing a respective disease. The targets of most drugs are proteins. The drug molecule, which is supposed to cure the respective disease, inserts itself into a functionally important crevice of the target protein, like a key in a lock. The drug molecule is then connected to the target and either induces or, more commonly, inhibits the protein's normal function.

| | |
|---|---|
| Toxicogenomics | Application of genetic and genomic methods to the study of toxicology. |
| Toxicology | Study of poisonous substances in terms of their chemistry, effects, and treatments. |
| Treatment Investigational New Drug | An Investigational New Drug that makes a promising new drug available to desperately ill patients as early in the drug development process as available. The FDA permits the drug to be used if there is preliminary evidence of efficacy and it treats a serious or life-threatening disease, or if there is no comparable therapy available. |
| Vaccine | An agent containing antigens. It is used for stimulating the immune system of the recipient to produce specific antibodies providing active immunity and/or passive immunity in the progeny. |

# Authors

**Prof. Dr. Oliver Gassmann** is Professor of Technology Management and Director at the Institute of Technology Management at the University of St. Gallen, Switzerland, since 2002. Between 1996 and 2002 he worked for Schindler and led its Corporate Research for the group as Vice President Technology Management.

Today he serves on several boards, e.g., the editorial board of R&D Management Journal, BGW St. Gallen-Vienna (co-founder), Zühlke Technology Group (board member), GLORAD Research Center Bejing-St. Gallen (co-director), the national committee for science and research (Economie-suisse), Project Management Academy (chairman), Schindler (member of audit committee), HSG Research Committee (president). He is active in research, executive education, and consulting for several multinational companies.

Oliver Gassmann holds a master's degree in business and economics from the University of Hohenheim, Germany, and received a Ph.D with highest distinction from the University of St. Gallen. He has published 11 books as author, co-author and editor, and over 160 publications on management of technology and innovation in leading journals. In 1998, he was awarded with the RADMA prize. His work has been published in English, German, French, Chinese, and Japanese.

**Dr. Gerrit Reepmeyer** is currently working as a healthcare consultant in the United States. From 2004 to 2006, he was a Visiting Scholar at Columbia Business School in New York, where he received research grants from the Swiss National Science Foundation to conduct research on innovation management and licensing with a focus on the pharmaceutical industry. Prior to that, Gerrit Reepmeyer was a Research Associate at the Institute of Technology Management at the University of St. Gallen in Switzerland. Before joining the Institute of Technology Management in St. Gallen, he worked in the position of a Manager with the venture capital firm KnowledgeCube Group, Inc. in New York.

Gerrit Reepmeyer received his Doctor of Business Administration with summa cum laude from the University of St. Gallen in 2005, and he holds a master's degree in business & engineering from Technical University

Berlin, Germany, as well as a Master of Science in Management from Stevens Institute of Technology, US. While studying in the United States, he was a scholar of the German Academic Exchange Service (DAAD).

Gerrit Reepmeyer has authored three books, five book chapters and over 15 articles on pharmaceutical R&D management as well as the impact of demographics on innovation management.

**Prof. Dr. Maximilian von Zedtwitz** is a Professor of Innovation Management at several universities in China and Europe, including Tsinghua University in Beijing, the University of St. Gallen in Switzerland, and the School of Management in Grenoble. Previously, he was a Professor at IMD, Lausanne, and a Visiting Fellow at Harvard University, Cambridge, Massachusetts. With Oliver Gassmann, he leads the GLORAD Research center between the University of St. Gallen and Tsinghua. He is also president of AsiaCompete Int'l Ltd., a firm specializing on technology intelligence and innovation scouting in China, with offices in Hong Kong, Shanghai, and Beijing. Furthermore, he serves on the boards of several technology-intensive firms and organizations.

Max von Zedtwitz teaches innovation and R&D management, China-business, and technology-based incubation in MBA, Ph.D., and executive education programs. Having published more than 50 articles in leading practitioner and academic journals and eight books, he has won several awards for research excellence and publications. He serves on the editorial boards of R&D Management, the Journal of International Management, and Technological Analysis and Strategic Management, and several other international journals reporting research on innovation, entrepreneurship, and technology management.

Printing: Krips bv, Meppel, The Netherlands
Binding: Stürtz, Würzburg, Germany